FACE II FACE

SAMAJESTY STARR

Pure Thoughts Publishing, LLC

© Copyright 2015 by Sam "Samajesty" Vaughn

All rights reserved.

This document is geared towards providing exact and reliable information in regards to the topic and issue covered. The publication is sold with the idea that the publisher is not required to render accounting, officially permitted, or otherwise qualified services. If advice is necessary, legal or professional, a practiced individual in the profession should be consulted from a Declaration of Principles which has been accepted and approved equally by a Committee of the American Bar Association and a Committee of Publishers and Associations.

In no way is it legal to reproduce, duplicate, or transmit any part of this document, in either electronic means or in printed format. Recording of this publication is strictly prohibited, and any storage of this document is not allowed except with written permission from the publisher. All rights reserved.

The information provided herein is stated to be truthful and consistent, in that any liability, in terms of inattention or otherwise, by any usage or abuse of any policies, processes, or directions contained within is the solitary and utter responsibility of the recipient reader. Under no circumstances will any legal responsibility or blame be held against the publisher for any reparation, damages, or monetary loss due to the information herein, either directly or indirectly.
Respective authors own all copyrights not held by the publisher.

The information herein is offered solely for informational

purposes, and is universal as so. The presentation of the information is without contract or any type of guarantee assurance.

The trademarks that are used are without any consent, and the publication of the trademark is without permission or backing by the trademark owner. All trademarks and brands within this book are for clarifying purposes only and are the owned by the owners themselves, not affiliated with this document.

All Scripture quotation, unless otherwise indicated, are taken from the Holy Bible, New International Version®. NIV®. Copyright © 1973, 1978, 1984 by International Bible Society. Used by permission of Zondervan Publishing House.

ISBN: 978-1-943409-06-8

All rights reserved

Dedication

This book is dedicated to God first and foremost. He orchestrated every step of the way for my good and understanding, even when I didn't think I was good or I didn't understand.

It is also dedicated to everyone I encountered on this journey, whether you know it or not you were a part of my life and this process. For the record I harbor no ill feelings toward anyone! In order for me to get my healing I had to share my testimony! It's all a part of the growth process!

Finally to those who try so hard to be perfect the truth is you cannot be. You can learn how to embrace all of you! The good, bad, and the ugly! Find the balance and Live... Know that God loves all of you.....Just the way you are!

Contents

Chapter 1 "Da City"..5

Chapter 2 "This Is for You"..14

Chapter 3 "Fire"..24

Chapter 4 "It Was You"..34

Chapter 6 "It's Ya Birthday"...55

Chapter 7 "Gimme Some Room"..65

Chapter 8 "Mrs. Perfect"..78

Chapter 9 "Ultimatum"...93

Chapter 10 "Goin All Out"...106

Chapter 11 "Remember My Name"...119

Chapter 12 "It's On!!!"...128

About the Author..139

Chapter 1 "Da City"

There is a state that is part of the Ohio Valley, located in the Midwest region of the United States of America. A state through which the Ohio River flows and its current washes the dead wildlife that's been poisoned by the high contamination of pollution upon its muddy banks. It's considered a transport state because its geographical position is almost centered in America and from its highways you can travel in any direction potentially navigating to any location in the U.S.A. It's not just the home of the U.S. Armory's treasury, where supposedly the Federals house all the gold of Fort Knox. However, just like the great author/song composer Stephen Foster wrote in the 1800's, it is "My Ole Kentucky Home." Commonly referred to or known as the Bluegrass state. If you are curious as to why it's nicknamed that, in the Spring/Summer months the rural fields landscaping is very beautiful, the shrubbery is so green and healthy it appears to have a bluish tint to it. Which sounds good in theory or general conversation however, the validity of the phrase I can't speak on because that's a totally different Kentucky then the one I am familiar with. My career choice has provided many opportunities to visit a lot of different cities in this beautiful country and it always surprises me how many people I meet who've never heard of Louisville, KY. Or many others whose never heard of The Kentucky Derby (which is the oldest consecutive sporting event in American history). It always gives me great joy to inform them of this prestigious international equestrian event. Typically, people respond in ridicule because society has painted a picture of equestrianism to be an activity strictly for Caucasians. Only to find out from me, that African Americans were the originators of this sporting event as slaves, because it was their duty to tend to the horses, many of the original Derby jockeys and winners were black men. The bad side of this history lesson is it normally doesn't help with people of big city mindsets, who stereotype all Kentuckians as uneducated, barefoot horseback riders, wearing cowboy hats and galloping down a dirt road. This is normally when the parameters of my lecture expands to become more metropolitan lifestyle inclusive. My dissertation pretty much always begins like this!

I'm from the sixteenth largest city in the United States of America. Named after King Louis XVI of France and founded in 1778 by George Rogers Clark. It is the world renown home of the Kentucky Derby housed by Churchill Downs, and the official home of the Louisville Slugger Bat which both date back to the late 1800's. These are just a few of the historical monuments from my experiences and research that are international and have operated over a century adding to the legacy of this great city, however let us discuss the Louisville Key; I speak of when I scream, "I'm from Da City!" It comes as a surprise to most fans and followers when they discover, although Louisville is my proclaimed hometown, it is not my place of birth. I was born in a Military Hospital on an army base called Fort Benning, right outside of the city of Columbus, Georgia. However most of my formative and grooming years were spent in Da City (Louisville). This is where the majority of my known biological kinfolk were born, lived, and many still reside today. Most of which will tell you the first sign of a true Kentuckian is having a preference or favorite collegiate athletic team in the ongoing rivalry between the Louisville Cardinals and the Kentucky Wildcats. Most of the younger generation who's in to gangbanging normally pick their squad by the neighborhood or set colors. The Cardinal colors are red and black which are widely known as Blood colors, a street gang, in various neighborhoods in America. While the Wildcat colors are Blue and white which are widely known as Crips' colors, a street gang, in various neighborhoods in America. For this reason one must be careful while touring or passing through certain neighborhoods in Da' City, wearing certain colors or supporting certain teams because the local gangbangers may mistake your identity. There are many other local gangs and cliques but these are generally the only two who create confrontations over colors. Keep that in mind when passing through but the real beef in the state of Kentucky is the well known rivalry between the Cardinals and the Wildcats, which just about every real resident has chosen a side and boastfully represents it.

No disrespect intended to my University of Kentucky Wildcat fans, "Go Big Blue." However early in my adolescence, I was raised by my elders who came up during the post-slavery era. These ancestors of mine grew up fighting the arrogant, ignorance of the brutally violent, and prejudice, racist confederate south. Although positioned in the Mid-West region and historically proclaimed to be neutral, Kentucky and Indiana were a part of, or aided, the Confederacy. That's why racism, which has yet to be completely eradicated still runs much deeper here than most Mid-Western or North American states. The evidence is obvious and visible. Hence Kentucky's symbol of the commonwealth is the French, Fleur-de-lis. This is a French lily-like flower that represents the original 13 colonies of America. The original 13 colonies that enslaved brutalized and oppressed our African and Native American ancestors. In my personal opinion, the Kentucky state flag is blue with the oppression and pain of my ancestors, with the French and British gentleman shaking hands in unification, agreeing to be each other's allies against all who doesn't look like them. For when they formed this commonwealth alliance, the wealth or welfare of people of color could not be taking consideration, because we weren't commoners. Per our Bill of Rights and Constitution of the United States of America, slaves and or people of color individually wasn't considered a whole man, but only 3/5's of a man. That's one of life's true mysteries and untold stories of a country's deceit and betrayal of their own people.

During the Civil War there was a promotional deal for slaves to join the Northern Union and fight against the confederate south. The original agreement offered was not only freedom from slavery but also forty acres of land and a mule for each solider. Faithfully these brothers enlisted, fought, and died claiming a triumphant victory for the Union that would have been impossible to acquire without their assistance. There isn't a record of how many colored soldiers from what family bloodlines signed up and agreed to the deal, however if there was it would be difficult to trace since most slaves were given new names by their owners, and it was typically strictly prohibited for slaves to read and write. This means that similar to the operations of the music industry of today, brothers were told what the contract was supposed to say, what they would receive and where to sign. After all of the battlegrounds soil was fertilized with the blood and motionless bodies of our ancestors. When the smoke cleared and the dust settled not one acre of land, or a mule, not even a puppy, just some fine print in the constitution stating you're not a slave anymore, but you're also not yet considered a man. Our ancestors were not allowed to vote or even give a valid testimony in court without a witness because legally (which still haven't been changed) people of color are documented as three-fifths of a man. Since its very existence, America's had an ongoing fight with oppression, equality, civil rights, and has progressed to the point of having a president of color. Yet our most sacred national documents and records haven't been changed to reflect our unified progression?

As you're reading this allow me to present a question for your intellectual consideration, How do you measure a man? I never understood who had the power to do so or what scales were used to measure a man. Likewise with all due respect, I never understood how the sixteenth President of the United States of America Abraham Lincoln still today receives credit as the liberator of our people. When in his personal memoirs he stated himself, "If I can keep the union intact and defeat the south without freeing one slave I will."

Please understand me when I say this, my goal is not to pass judgment on anyone, nor do I intend to tarnish the image of our great country or its written founding fathers and leaders. These statements may seem harsh and hard to believe but for the record I am not nor have I ever been a racist! I just happen to know some hard truths and I am not scared or ashamed to share them. Yes, as a Black/African American man, the actual history, struggle and legacy of my people in this country affects me in many ways. Also there is a natural inclination to love all those who share my pigment and for those who are aware of the struggle, my pain. Yet as a follower of Christ and believer of God, I feel it's mandatory and automatic that I love all of his children. For whatever color your skin is, we all are created by the one true King in his image, and as his children. That' what makes each one of us royalty and so I address you as such, when I greet you… "Sire...or ya Majesty"

I said all that to say I understood the pain behind my elders despise of the University of Kentucky because of segregation they couldn't attend this University, so the University of Louisville was erected to pacify and silence, the screams of discrimination by masses of colored people who yearned for knowledge and desired to be educated (L1C4). My earliest memories of passion stirring up for Da City, is when the Louisville Cardinals basketball team was on the court.

Like many Black-American families in the 1980's 90's, mine would gather at one members' house like a family reunion. We would rally around that old, wooden, 27 inch, floor model television set with the broken knobs and cheer on our Cardinals. I had so much love for my Cardinals missing a game would make me feel guilty, like grandma made me feel when I missed church on Sunday mornings. I'm talking so much love that when the Cardinals lost their games, I would sit in my bedroom on my scratched up cherry wood bunk bed set and soil my Mickey Mouse fantasia bedroom sheets with youthful tears. That's when I first begin to fall in love with Da City (Louisville). Head Coach Denny Crum and the Cardinal basketball team made me laugh, cry, and cheer until I didn't have a voice. From that moment on I was, still am, and forever will be a Louisvillian.

As I matured from my adolescence into my pre-teenage years, I acquired a wealth of knowledge from Da City. Being ambidextrous and gifted I learned to balance my scholastic and street knowledge well. Maintaining honors status quarterly at school yet somehow keeping the beginnings of my street credit intact. Thanks to my now belated cousin, Robert Lamonte Silver, who we called Monte.

Monte showed me how to Rap, before understudying him in hip-hop, everything I attempted to create came out like a poem or R&B song. If not for the basics and fundamentals he taught me about the art form I would've never been able to create a career of longevity with this craft. I can still picture him dancing around the house, in a Cross Colors outfit, lack Kangol, and Locs sunglasses. In an instant he'll stop dancing, lift up his Locs, staring at you with these big, deep, dark brown eyes and say, "Give me something!" Now take into consideration Monte was probably 6 foot 2 inches tall, with a finely toned muscular physique. He was the known leader of the feared and revered local gang, The Geek Boys. His alias was Hardcore, and he was known for being just that…hardcore! So when Monte asked you for something, you felt a sense of urgency, to deliver his request. The good thing for me was when he said "Give me something!" he meant a concept, a subject, or really just one word. Because he was so talented all he needed was for you to say the first word that came to your mind, and by the time the last syllable rolled off your tongue. He would be vocally creating a freestyle composition off your one word and he would always complete the verse not stop because he messed up. That's where my passion for creative writing and performing came from. Monte passed March 17, 1993, at the age of 22. This was an event that shook me at my core and changed the course of my life. That year at 12 years of age, I vowed to pursue our passion of music with all I had until I occupied a cemetery grave plot like Monte.

As we reflect, my passion for Da City originated with the University of Louisville Athletics, my creative flow for Da City was adopted by the life and death of Robert Lamonte Silver, and my fighting pride for Da City should come as no surprise. For this man's an international celebrity, worldwide champion, motivator, activist, and so much more. My personal hometown hero was born Cassius Clay but widely known and respected as Muhammad Ali. I'm not going to go into details about his life because honestly all though I've met him, I don't know him or his family well enough to do so. I shouldn't have to anyway because you should already know his story. There are many books, movies, and documentaries that tell the inspirational, biographical facts of his life, which I encourage you to do your diligence and check them out. I assure you that no matter which story you read or video you view, you will truly be blessed by this visionary and powerful man of God. One fact that most people don't know about Ali is he was very instrumental in the liberation and full desegregation of not just Louisville KY; but America as a whole. Due to his personal beliefs and immovable stance on issues, from the war he refused to fight in, to the venues he refused to patronize because they were willing to accept his patronage but not other people of color. His athleticism coupled with his personality made all people love him, and his star power coupled with his personality made more people accept other people. That's the heart and pride of Da City, Louisville, KY.

Now is there violence in Da City? Yes…..Louisville averages double the National rate of violent crimes, double the National rate of murder/manslaughter, and almost three times the national rate of robbery. High School drop-outs, drugs, and homelessness are at an all time high and rising. However that's not the vision of my city I would like to magnify or glorify. I assure you that wherever you go in this great country of ours you'll probably find the same horrifying statistics. What brought me out and over was God. That coupled with the few motivational triggers of positivity that inspires and encourages me to continue propelling forward. No longer will I be distracted or discouraged by what other people or the media says about my city. I understand now that I solely have the responsibility to view and create my own ideology about who I am, what I am, where I live, and what it all means to me. That way nobody can convince me to be stagnated or complacent by sowing seeds of negativity into my life out of their own fear and insecurities. For I was not given the spirit of fear but of power, love and a sound mind. For the record remember that about 90% of the battles we face are mental. It's not what happens to you but how you respond and react when things happen to you. Louisville is where everything originally started happening to and for me so it'll always be my favorite place in the world.

"…We Go Hard! / I'm from Da' city, Da' city, Derby City" and cheers to you Louisville, KY… *"Go Baby, Go Baby, Go!"*

Chapter 2 "This Is for You"

"Excuse me young man, my name is George Sutton and I was told that I could find a guy named Saint Majestic Star around here. Would you happen to know him? Or have an idea where I could find a guy who raps named Saint Majestic Star?"

I remember being asked this question on a beautiful autumn afternoon, as I stood outside of the physical therapy rehabilitation clinic that I worked for at the time. Reluctant to answer the question without knowing who this stranger was, I first eyeballed this elder gentleman and sized him up. He stood about 5 foot 10 inches tall, slender built with a little beer gut. He had a dark copper colored skin tone, with a small salt and pepper afro, and a matching old school wide and very thick mustache. I paused in confusion staring at him from under my hand, that I was using as a visor to block the sun from the eyes, asking myself "Who is this guy, and what does he want with me?" I had already ruled out the police because he was dressed in a black and white fresh tailored suit with a matching wide brim Godfather hat. Not to mention he asked for me by my stage name, this meant he couldn't have been a radical evangelical or a Jehovah Witness.

All of these thoughts and concerns sprinted across the axis of my mind which was spinning expeditiously. Every heart I had broken and every crime I ever committed crossed my mind as I prepared to defend myself, wondering if this gentleman sought me out for retribution of one of my past victims. Finally my anxiety settled, curiosity took over and reluctantly I answered, "The name is SaMajesty Starr, and I am him, Sire." Within an instant, I witness the expression on his face go from a frustrated curiosity, to an overwhelming elation. Before any other words were uttered between the two of us, this brother embraced me in his arms as if we were long lost distant relatives. As awkward as it may sound, I was comforted by his hug and felt assured that in no way did he come to harm me nor even bring me bad news. Focused like the good student who sits in the very front of the classroom, I paid close attention and didn't say a word hoping to have all of the questions that I was silently asking myself answered. Instantly, Mr. Sutton whom I called George opened his mouth and within 20 minutes I knew everything that I felt I needed to know. George was an executive music producer/artists manager, who in his past had a couple of shots at the majors in the music industry. Out of respect for him I won't mention any of his groups or artists names but through the story he told me, they all had one thing in common. At some point in their career after collaborating with him, either right before signing their big deal or right after signing their big deal they each fired him. Heartbroken and discouraged he had spent the past ten years running from the music industry. He explained his perspective of the music business as more than just a way to raise his family above the average/middle class income status, but also as his calling and purpose in life.

While attending a Baptist Church service on a Sunday morning in Louisville, KY; George discerned a word was speaking to his spirit through the pastor's sermon. This word not only caused him to reflect but it also liberated him from his past career woes as it related to the music industry, and motivated him to take one last chance at managing/producing artist. After the benediction of that worship service, George sat in the sanctuary for a couple of hours praying unto the Lord. While he was still in between the church pews, he was approached by three associate ministers, who'd been fellowshipping in the vestibule, and was curious to see if he needed some assistance. George began to testify, sharing with the ministers the story of his past and how the preached word that morning touched his soul breathing new life into him. After all he'd been through in the music industry and all the years he spent away from the business, he felt a spiritual unction to return and face what he once ran from. He asked them if there was someone in the gospel music scene locally who may be able to benefit from his previous knowledge and experiences in the music world. George said, "I took it as a sign of the Lord, because simultaneously almost in unison they all said SaMajesty Starr," and I thought to myself, "Damn this guy must be really good!" The only problem was none of the ministers knew where I could be found outside of the sanctuary on Sunday mornings.

To what extent George went through in order to gain access to the necessary information that allowed him to find me, I'll never know. However, I count it as a blessing from God this elderly man would go through so many changes to find me, only to share his experiences, gifts, and talents with the sole intent of assisting me in the forward progression of my music/ministry. Not to mention George had more energy and passion that I had seen or felt in years. I honestly believe that he was an angel of the Lord sent to me during a dark season, when I was depressed, discouraged, and wanted to give up. I really needed the inspiration, so like a sponge under a running water faucet, I began to feel rejuvenated by soaking up all the zeal that I felt permeating from George's spirit. We became business partners in the music industry but more importantly, we became really good friends. George took the time to get close enough to really know me. Everything from my desire to please God to my not so secret sins I battled with daily. George never condoned nor supported any of my self-destructive behaviors. However, he never judged nor condemned me for them neither. No matter how big the stage or audience got, he always respected me as a man first and never put my gifting above my family or well-being. This made me respect George so much more because until that point in my career as a Holy Hip-Hop artist I was accustomed to being brought into church services, community events, and inspirational venues only to share my gifts and talents with the people.

There weren't many times that I can recall as a leader in ministry were my personal lifestyle was ever a major concern. There were times, when I publicly had more than one intimate relationship in the same church and ministered through song during a worship service while I was under the influence of drugs or alcohol. This is not something that I brag about, actually it's one of the shameful and painful memories I've buried deep in my repentance files. The message that I aim to convey by bringing it up is that, I spent so much time, trying to save everyone else's children, that I myself was sinking in sin and paving my own way to hell. Most of the congregation didn't know and most spiritual leaders didn't care as long as I continued to bring more youth and tithing /offering dollars into their collection plates. I was officially in the fight of my life and George witnessed it all. This is where the concept of the album, "Face 2 Face", originated from. George was my corner man. He kept saying, "I don't care if you continue to do Gospel music or go back to doing street music, either way I'm going to support you 100%! However, I need you to understand that you won't be free, saved, or happy until you learn to stop worrying about others and what they think. You've got to learn to be you!"

I can't recall how many times I heard that lecture during my identity crisis period when I was soul searching to find me. All glory to God, I found myself through finding Christ, who washed my sins and gave me a second chance at life. However, I now understand that Salvation is a process of transitions, in which daily we must battle our natural fleshly sin sick selves. Renewing our minds and purging our hearts to become more like Jesus Christ, if we believe in him and accept him as our personal Lord and Savior. This is the main idea and underline conceptual theme behind the album, "Face 2 Face."

It was late in the evening on a cold Thursday in the middle of January. George came by the house, and was ecstatic about what he considered, "Our Big Shot!" By day, George was a bus driver for the Jefferson county public school system and felt compelled to do something positive for the special needs children whom he witnessed every day on the job. His idea was to create a song for the WHAS Crusade for children which is a non-profit organization who's committed to aiding and assisting children with special needs. George requested that I create a song that we could share with the organization and all who's affiliated with it, in order to raise awareness and help generate donations for their cause. This concept gave birth to a philosophy that we still utilize in our company operations today:

"You can't bless the people of God (especially children) and God not bless you. Don't always be in search of dollar signs because some of the best payments you'll receive won't be monetary."

There will be many times in your professional career or social life that you will connect with different people whom it'll behoove you to assist in their journey. By blessing them with your gifts, time, talent, expressions, or presence in some shape, form or fashion it always comes back and it's not always in cash. It may not come back as fast as you sent it out, or the same way that you sent it out. Be careful not to set yourself up in thinking that this concept should be mutually expressed because it might not even come back through the same person you gave it to. Idealistically, the rule would be to follow the unction in your spirit (gut), to just do what you know is right, the way you would want somebody to do it for you, without expectations of receiving anything, and pray you've blessed someone else. In my experiences this creates the largest potential spiritual blessing/reward once the seed is sown in faith and the harvest manifests. Remember cash is only king if you don't know

Y'eshua the king of kings. George said, "Sam, you make the song and God's going to get us right through them doors! I got my people in place waiting on the product, just make the song right now and we will get back to the rest of the album later."

The next day we went to a production/recording studio on 38th street in the west end of Da' City. We met with a phenomenal producer/engineer named GT also known as G#, who was known around Da' City as one of the elite creative musical minds that you could hire. George and I walked into the production room, where GT sat in front of a Phantom keyboard workstation that had a midi line running to an Apple Mac computer, and an adobe studio program was visible on the monitor screen. This was not my first time meeting or working with GT, we both understood each other's routine and work ethics so conversation was to a minimum. I started explaining to GT the concept of the song, along with its purpose and what we were attempting to do. He just smiled replying in his signature low pitched, whisper toned, humble voice saying, "Yea, I got you! Uh…all I need is uh… $75 and about 30 minutes. Do you have a hook for the song already? How does the chorus go?" I started reciting this chant that my wife (Cherrie) and I had been working on,

"This is for you / for you / for you. / This is for me / for me / for me / and all the children in need."

And within 20-25 minutes the air was cloudy with various types of smoke but the entire instrumentation for the song was complete. Over the next couple of days Cherrie and I would listen to this instrumental repeatedly. I call this process, vibing, where throughout your normal daily routine you consistently listen to the musical composition without writing or reciting any lyrics. The idea behind this process is trying to mesh the feeling of the concept with the vibration of the instrumental to create a unified musical sentiment that coordinates and compliments one another. During the vibing process some form of inspiration is typically used to enhance the emotion, make it personal and relatable while expediting the creative process. On this particular project, pictures, thoughts and memories of every mildly to seriously handicapped person I'd ever encountered was used. Then, with the help of Angel Pointer (my cousin by marriage) I was able to connect with the good people of Peak Community services where she's employed. Peak community services is a facility and program that provides support services for individual with intellectual and developmental disabilities. Finally, I researched any and every available piece of information I could find on the WHAS Crusade for Children. Vibing over all this compiled information data it didn't take long at all to complete the writing process for this song. Cherrie and I decided to solicit some help from the producer GT and Tierria Pointer, (my wife's sister), on the background vocals, and the WHAS Crusade for children song, "This Is for You," was complete.

    The comical part was George didn't have one connect that could, "Get us through them doors," as he claimed. We didn't waste time getting frustrated because now the song was complete and all-glory-to-God Cherrie had assisted one of WHAS's anchors with a local news top story. The anchor's name was Renee Murphy and Cherrie had built a strong enough rapport with her that they exchanged numbers and became friends. Renee told Cherrie that if she ever needed anything to give her a call so without hesitation Cherrie called her and told her about the song. Renee happily organized a meeting that consisted of Dawn Lee, CEO of the Crusade for Children, and the two main producers of the annual televised campaign. Introductions were made, music was played, hands were shook, and we left the television station as the newest members of the WHAS Crusade for Children artists. Which we still participate in as our schedule permits each year. However, we're currently discussing the beginning and the first year we participated in the Crusade for Children event was bittersweet. I say this because not only was my wife pregnant and due to go into labor at anytime, but also George didn't show and I hadn't heard from him in weeks prior to the date. It was an emotional blow that struck me pretty hard because finally our time to shine had come, after months of praying, laboring, and preparing for this one moment. This opportunity would be an internationally streamed and regionally televised live performance and I would have to proficiently complete it without even a telephone call from George. Not to mention I had been calling and searching for him for weeks to No avail. All Glory to God the performance went well and our second son Emmanuel Da Promise was born the following day. Finally things were looking good for our company. I didn't know what to make of George's recent absences, and I tried not to fear for the worst although I knew I had to continue moving forward.

Months passed by without hearing from George until one day I was running errands and noticed his car parked outside of GT's studio. I wanted to drive on pass, and ignore his presence in the neighborhood just like he had ignored all my attempts to contact him but I couldn't. For closure or whatever reason, I felt that I just had to know what happened to the air-tight solidified bond of our friendship. Did I do something that I deserved to be ignored for? Was he going through something so personal, that even though I was vulnerable and transparent enough to be an open book for him, he couldn't share it with me?

In retrospect, none of these questions really mattered because I wasn't concerned with the answers to them. Honestly, I was so hurt that I couldn't compose myself long enough to be civilized and calmly ask the questions I desired to know. My emotions completely took over the very minute I crossed the threshold of the studio and our eyes met. I wasn't ridiculously belligerent, vulgar, violent, or physically threatening at all. However, I was harsh, rude, and blatantly disrespectful while conveying my message in an attempt to vocalize or communicate my pain. I could tell that George was shocked by my behavior and his feelings were hurt. However, at the time I was also hurting from the months of worrying about his well-being and fearing that he was dead. Those thoughts had turned into anger once I saw he was alright and realized that he was just ignoring me, only made me want to hurt him too! I guess the old saying, "hurting people, hurt people," is true.

It took a long time after that verbal altercation, for the spirit of conviction to resonate in my soul so strongly that I felt compelled to call him. It would be almost a year later before we actually engaged in a conversation, in which we spoke casually about his recent health issues and what I'd been doing with the music in his absence. The verbal confrontation that took place at the studio, or the reason for it was never a topic discussion. It was almost like we picked up where we left off before the first Crusade for Children event and the altercation never happened. We both agreed to meet up and catch up on old times but we never got the chance. I received an email about a month later that had an attachment of a WHAS local news top story. The story told of an elder gentleman named George Sutton, who seemingly had a heart attack while driving on the highway, crashed into the median, and was ejected from his car. He died at the scene of the accident, and they had graphic pictures that showed the detailed damage to his car along with his lifeless body being transported to the emergency room. The moral of this story is……don't waste precious minutes of your life angry or harboring negativity. Because someone could be unexpectedly silenced forever, while your throwing your temper tantrum and giving them the silent treatment. I still temporarily deal with some of that guilt because we never got the chance to apologize or air it all out. I feel eternally indebted to George and his family for the sacrifice and struggles they made for my growth and progression. Obviously God called him home, so I can't be upset about that, however I just hope he knows that I love him, I'm sorry, and I'm very grateful for his impact on and in my life. If you can hear from beyond the grave, Sire, "I'm Gon' Get Us Through Dem' Doors," and every time that WHAS Crusade for Children song is played or performed anywhere…..This Is for You!!!

Chapter 3 "Fire"

Before I actually began writing to the instrumental for this production, initially in the creative process, it was going to be a promiscuous dance song called, "Roll." The logic behind that concept stemmed from a promiscuous female friend of mine, whom at the time was employed at a Hooters restaurant in Southern Indiana. Hooters, is a sports bar that I used to patronize when I found myself stressed, depressed, or frustrated and fighting a bad case of writers block. If I had to be honest because of my prestigious community status and who I proclaimed to be, this was the closest I could get to a strip club without tarnishing my image and reputation. Like most men, I always wanted to be wherever decent looking, half-dressed women were. Especially women who are happy to see you, fully attentive in your presence and catering to your every beckon call. Even if you have to pay them to do so, it still boosts your self-confidence, male ego, and chauvinistic pride. So for the ladies who are reading this chapter, this may be the reason your man frequents what you may consider raunchy establishments, and I'm willing to debate the argument that most men feel like they perform better in the presence of attractive females. Whatever a man does as a profession, hobby, or recreation if you strategically place a hot chick in the vicinity I guarantee you'll see an improvement or adjustment in his attitude, character, overall performance and/or work ethic. In my personal opinion, the only exceptions to this theory would be for homosexual men and men who're too infatuated or intimidated by an alluring woman to perform at all. I could be wrong, but this is a concept that I feel I've learned through experience in my pre-salvation days.

Back when I was a whoremonger under the misconception that I was pimping, life taught me that in reality I was prostituting myself and others. I worked with different models, dancers, and prostitutes who understood what the gift of gab mixed with the power of the law of attraction could do. I've witnessed on many occasions people be swindled, teased, manipulated or literally screwed out of their livelihood. The fact of the matter is, we all as human beings are flawed and carry a void within us that most people don't know about. The skill behind being an effective pimp is to exploit the flaw yet fill the void and make the victim so comfortable that they no longer believe they're a victim. For example, there was a female from our neighborhood named Christina. Christina was a pretty young lady with low self-esteem and even though she was a people pleaser, she had no friends. The first thing I did was filled the void by become her best friend. I allowed her to know that people didn't like her because they were haters who couldn't stand to see her shine, and we should give her a hood name that matched her character (Crystal). I spent some time with Crystal, sharing with her my ideas, beliefs, principles, and street knowledge. Some of this information would be genuine but the bulk of it would be a fabrication of the truth in order to sway her through the process of initiation so together we could re-invent her identity. I told her we would be friends no matter what and she could always count on me to be there in her times of need. During this period of building trust she shared with me how men would take advantage of her sexually because she didn't like to upset people and had a problem saying no. I taught Crystal to say, "Yes, but can you…?" and "Sure, if you'll…?" I told her as her friend she had to stop letting these guys walk all over her, if she was going to be used then they would be also, and she had a problem with any of them contact me. I set some realistic goals that we could achieve and enjoy together if she stuck to the plan and I kept my word on mostly everything I told her.

"It's going to happen anyway, might as well get some money for it!" This was a slogan I used constantly to justify my actions and make me feel better about successful solicitations in sex trafficking. The law of attraction is alive and real, depending on who possesses its power and how they use it could determine peace or chaos (liberation or enslavement). I say this because the gift of gab and the law of attraction usually go hand and hand. For what you are drawn to by attraction usually carries an automatic seductive swagger that's so magnetic, you're hooked and involuntarily being reeled in with every line. You can say the law of attraction and the power of the tongue are equivalent in the respect of possessing the power of life and death. This is a very deep connection to tie together however as one who's effectively utilized these tactics for selfish gain and have witnessed the long term effects on victims, I know that statement to be true. I pray that anyone who was victimized or still being held captive by the misuse of my anointing, or shall I say the negative impact of my aura of attraction be healed and set free In the Name of Jesus! I also speak life and resurrection into the decaying bitter spirits of any zombie-like soul that in my time of identity crisis I attempted to slay with my tongue and left them for dead. May the spirit of the living Lord breathe and speak life into you as he did in the beginning of your journey, and utilize each one of us on our mission of kingdom building as we press toward the mark, Amen!

My alter ego, Klypto (klepto), still receives street credit in many ghetto neighborhoods as a pimp for these past sins I committed, which allowed me to adopt this self-destructive philosophy as part of my alias' character. The definition of a kleptomaniac is one who instinctively takes things from others without permission, thought, concern or regard. That is what I was known for… theft! I would steal money, merchandise, hearts, etc. If there was a way that I could benefit from pilferage in any form regardless of how much suffering it brought on the victim, I would take it! This is not a part of my past that I'm proud of, nor typically do I boast about. However in order to effectively tell this story, I feel it's mandatory that I give full disclosure while praying that my transparency helps save and liberate somebody else. This piece of information is very important because it displays the immaturity and fragility of my mindset, illustrating how I managed to get entangled in the very web I was weaving for others.

Now back to this Hooters Restaurant in Southern Indiana. I met quite a few Hooters girls in my time but not as many as I did during the season of creating "Face 2 Face". The reason being was it was a very challenging period of my life. My spiritual, mental, physical, and emotional health was shaky to say the least, putting all of my relationships business, personal and even marital on the rocks. This season was verbally indescribable however the best way I can attempt to sum it up was Insane! During this purging process I tried my hardest to isolate myself from all I knew and cared about, out of fear that I might hurt myself or someone else rather it would've been physically or emotionally. I wasn't willing to that risk so I would spend countless hours in establishments or sports bars like Hooters watching sporting events, drinking beer, and writing lyrics. "Fire" was different than the other tracks on the album because it was the only instrumental I received and couldn't figure out what to do with it. I found myself spending a lot of time drinking and vibing with this instrumental. The more time I spent in the establishment the more acquaintances and associates I built rapport with. Most of these acquaintances were patrons and some of them were employees of the establishment. One evening while sitting there going through my usual routine. I was introduced to a female server who transferred from an out-of-town location. In order to protect all parties involved including myself I will keep the names confidential and for the sake of telling the story we'll call her, Trouble. Trouble was a foreign exchange student from Florida by way of Brazil. She stood 5ft 5 inches tall, bowlegged and maybe one-hundred and forty pounds. She was a beautiful girl, pretty smile, with perfect teeth, long curly black hair, and a blemish-free butterscotch skin tone. From the moment she introduced herself as my waitress and I delayed my greeting because I was temporarily hypnotized by her sandy hazel eyes. At that moment, knowing I'm a happily married family man, who's a community/spiritual leader, and student of the gospel of Jesus Christ. I should have just got up and walked out. Especially given my past experience in relationships I spoke of earlier. The law of attraction was instantaneous, and powerful. Even though everything in my spirit told me to run, my flesh handicapped my physical body into a hypnotized paralytic state.

    Silently negotiating with myself, I made a promise. The agreement was as long as Trouble didn't make any flirtatious advancements towards me, then I wouldn't make any towards her. The plan was to ignore the lustful temptation stemming from the obvious magnetic attraction between Trouble and I, and focus strictly on the writing process I was already submerged in for the Face 2 Face Project. Unfortunately, after taking my order she returned not only with compliments but questions. Trouble pulled up a chair at my table and began inquiring about who I was, and what I was doing? Attempting to limit my conversation with her, I briefly answered the questions and asked her would she like to hear the instrumental for the song I was currently writing to, thinking she would decline and continue working. However, to my surprise she accepted my offer happily and began to joke with me about helping me write a hit song. I sarcastically accepted her offer, by replying. Come on let me see what you got! The instant she placed the ear buds in her ears, I pushed play on the disc player, and she had this sensual glare of admiration that arose temptation in me as she discreetly and seductively began dancing in front of me. She slowly moved her body from side to side and slightly rolled her hips with her legs together in a slight squatting position. This action drew the attention of everyone who caught a glimpse of the thirty second teaser she delivered in her movements. Immediately I stopped the music and silently reminded myself of a saying my friends and I would share with each other as married men:

"It may not mean anything, but it could cost you everything!"

She stopped dancing, smiled at me with the innocence of a toddler and a patron who was seated two tables over said, "Wow, Trouble! I like the way you roll!" After this patrons' line echoed in my head and I pictured Trouble repeating this dance and said, "That's it! That's the foundation of the chorus;

"I like the way she roll, Shorty / good as gold makes a brother lose control / every time she throws / I like the way she roll, roll, roll!"

Believing that I'd finally came up with the concept for the instrumental I began writing lyrics to it and building rapport with Trouble because she was the inspiration behind the song. At that point I started lying to myself, writing Trouble and my sinful flirtatious conversations off as business, attempting to make her believe she was justified in secretly coveting me because she was assisting me in fulfilling my purpose for life.

We exchanged numbers and began an inappropriate, but casual social relationship where we would talk on the phone and I would periodically come back to Hooters only during her work shifts to visit. Continuing to lie to myself I would say, "Sam we're not cheating, we've done nothing wrong! Trouble and I are just friends, and as long as there isn't any sexual contact involved we're good!" However the whole time I knew I was already in too deep. I knew that by continuing to play this little game, it would only be a matter of time before Trouble and my wife both would end up broken hearted. Unless I was able to be more compassionate instead of selfish so I could see the error of my ways, repent, and change. Having all the knowledge and experience I had in dating, pimping, and playing games I just couldn't bring myself to do the right thing. In retrospect I'm not sure if I really couldn't or if I was just being stubborn and didn't want to. Because the reality of the situation was I really liked Trouble, we shared some personal moments and became really close so I didn't want to see her hurt. However, I didn't want to lose the love of my life neither which also meant losing my family, business and ministry. Some may call it Karma, and some may call it the law of reaping and sowing. Either way, the same game that I used to master mind the demise of others while making a plush lifestyle for myself, had me engulfed in sin and wrapped in a lustful relationship that I just couldn't walk away from.

It was probably about two weeks later when my fantasy and nightmare merged. I walked in Hooters at about 10:00pm, on a beautiful breezy autumn night, knowing the dining area closed at midnight. I sat down in the same area I was accustomed to sitting in because it was the section where Trouble always served. I ordered a beer from another waitress and was disappointed because she informed me that Trouble got off early that night and was gone home. Being as Trouble told me earlier that her shift ended when the dining area closed, I was slightly worried that something may be wrong and why hadn't she called me. Just as I finished my drink and prepared to leave, Trouble walked up dressed as if she had a date that night. When she seen me gathering my items, paying the tab and preparing to leave, she made sure she caught my attention asking where we were going as if she had planned on accompanying me. Honestly, I was supposed to be on my way home to my family but couldn't pass on the opportunity for some alone time with Trouble, away from the security of the watchful eyes on her job. Before I knew it, we were riding in her car, drinking, flirting, frisking and planning a night of passion at a nearby hotel. We decided to make one stop prior to the hotel, a trip back across the bridge to Da' City so I could purchase a sack of hydroponic marijuana. We had planned to get high and have sex continuously in the order, until the morning so I called my weed man and asked him to meet me at a gas station in my old neighborhood. As we pulled into the location of the pre-arranged meeting, a fight broke out between two teenage black males right in front of her car. Luckily, this was my old stomping grounds, a neighborhood I was familiar with, well known in, and happened to know both of the young men who were violently engaged in the brawl. Against my better judgment I got out of the car and attempted to calm the altercation. Due to the fact that I'm a believer of Christ, even in a dark place where I'm about to sin myself I couldn't ignore this physical confrontation because I knew them and felt their blood would be on my hands if I stood by and did nothing. Standing right outside the front passenger door of her car, I talked to one of the brothers whom at that point were winning the fight, and ministered reconciliation begging for a truce. Not noticing the brother on the ground had slipped past us both, got to his gun and started shooting. Instinctively I prayed for peace and safety, yelling at the top of my lungs. "No weapon formed against me shall prosper. I believe in you God and your power to protect your children." Then I started praying for peace in the mind and love in the heart of the gunman. I continued praying for the failure of the devil's plan and the reinforcements of Holy angels. Fortunately everyone who was outside of the gas station before the shooting started had cleared out and no one was hurt. I was the only person left in the parking lot, except for Trouble whom I was staring at her completely shocked facial expression through the front windshield of her car. Hearing many tones of emergency sirens approaching, we did the same and got out of there quickly. I remember silently praising God, thinking of how embarrassing my life story would've been to end right there in the mess I was in. The fact that I was about to buy drugs and commit adultery would've over shadowed every good and positive thing I labored so hard to build.

As we traveled back to Indiana a conversation between us happened where she spoke of never being around someone so committed to saving others that they would risk their own life to ensure that the innocent bystanders as well as the perpetrators left unharmed. This conversation carried on for about an hour and as it shifted gears she began telling me about the last guy she was with. Discerning her pains, I could vision her future plans, the calling on her life and the real purpose of our relationship. I was reluctant to share with her what the spirit was saying because I secretly still wanted to go to the hotel. I tried to start smoking my weed hoping to dumb down the spirit and continue in my selfish plans of having one night of passion with this beautiful young lady. However as the effects of the marijuana kicked in, I fell into a deep meditational trance, and as I zoned out the entire night as well as the potential closure passed through my mind in visions and I begin to minister in spirit and truth to Trouble. Conviction filled both of our hearts as the truth was spoken, tears fell, and the decision to not go further in sin was mutually agreed upon. She drove me back to Hooters where my vehicle was parked. We hugged, thanked God, and I got out. The minute I got in my car, I begin to have ill feelings about the night because my flesh wanted to violate Trouble and my covenant with the Lord. Instantly I heard a voice speak in my head that only had one scriptural verse to recite in my spirit. That scripture was Jeremiah 20 verse 9;

"Then I said, I will not make mention of (the Lord) nor speak any more in His name. But his word was in mine heart as a burning fire shut up in my bones, and I was weary with forbearing, and I could not stay."

I was forced to reflect back to the night before. The lust of adultery, the anger of violence, and the hatred of murder was consumed in the fire of the spirit of our living Lord, Jesus the Christ. The revelation I received that morning was, even in the presence or process of sinning, the Lord will fill me with a uncontainable spiritual fire to do the right thing, so strong that regardless to what my flesh is screaming, I will be endowed with the power to consume it all in the fire of the Lord, and when I can't do it myself, if I hold my peace long enough he'll speak for me and do what he does best...... Save!

Chapter 4 "It Was You"

"It Was You" is one of those songs that can be hard to classify or place in a particular category. It has a Christian foundation but doesn't really quote any scriptures throughout the entire piece. It has a nice lyrical flow that's positive, conscious, and spiritual all at the same time. The vocals that are sung by my wife Queen Cherrie, have a deep soul classics feel, with a hint of modern gospel, and the instrumental music has a west coast Hip-Hop and R&B vibe lightly brushed over with a glaze of Jazz. For those who've never heard the song before, it is basically written in the form of a letter, and I'd have to say this is a love letter. This love letter is written in three parts, which are dedications to my wife, my children, and my God. The initial purpose of this song was to constantly remind others and myself of the main reasons I do what I do. More so myself, because when times get hard, money gets tight, and people get fickle, I needed something that could always bring me back to square one when I got too far ahead of myself, when it seems like everyone is against me, or when I just don't want to do this anymore. This love letter would always remind me that I do it for love, because I love, and always will be loved! Therefore, I don't have to put too much emphasis on people pleasing or worrying about how I'm received or perceived to be. The hook of this song says,

"I know I don't say it enough but I love you / no matter how far we apart I'm thinking of you / just put this on repeat when I can't speak or touch you / and know that if I ever met love then it was you!"

While at the same time in the background the chorus of the song sings,

"If I ever met love before it was you."

For those of you reading this chapter right now, can you honestly say that you've ever really been loved? Can you honestly say that there is at least one person that you know without a shadow of a doubt that you love? Well, for me this letter is the evidence of love and that is the sole purpose this song serves.

"It was you," Cherrie Pointer who met a young man that was all over the place. Confused about what he wanted to do and be in his life, because he wasn't sure if he wanted to be the bad guy or the good guy. When I was at my worst, you accepted me. You saw in me then, what I'm just now beginning to see in myself. You encouraged and motivated me to keep pressing forward even when I didn't want to. You've never given up on me, even when I've tried to push you away. You've allowed me to be me, and accepted everything that comes along with my character, good and bad. Baby, you believe in me sometimes more than I believe in myself and you love me so much, it's impossible not to love myself. "It was you" who helped me chip away at stone in my chest, until the jewel that lied underneath came forth, and allowed me to be the person that I am today. Thank you so much for just being you, you are my greatest gift from God and I love you!

"It was you," all of my seeds that have budded and are beginning to bloom so that one day you'll be flowers that bring beauty to the global landscape of the Earth. My children are the ones who always make me feel good, no matter how rough the day has been for me. Just the genuine love and joy they express to me during every visitor conversation. It amazes me how they watch me in close examination of my every word, and action as students taking notes from their legendary idol. No matter what the world may think of me, to my kids I'm the greatest, and regardless of what you say about me, I can do no wrong in the eyes of my children. "It was you," that came into this Earth trusting and depending on me to make a way for us. You gave me a sense of entitlement, as well as a sense of responsibility, a sixth sense, and common sense for that matter (lol). You are the proof that I will have a future here on this Earth and every decision that I make is crucial. We are connected by spirit so when you hurt, I hurt, when you smile, I smile and I still can't explain it but there is something truly magical about the hugs you give me. All of you are my best blessings from God, my biggest investment and deposit into the Earth! I love you...

As the saying goes, I saved the best for last! "It was you," God, who in the beginning gave your only begotten son, so that I may not perish but have ever lasting life, if I only believe! You knew and loved me that much before my parents even had an inkling of an idea that I would exist. You kept a watchful eye over me, as you allowed me to make my own decisions and create my own course of life. You did this knowing the whole time that the good and bad would work together if I truly loved you, so this was all character building in my process of becoming what you already knew I was and destined me to be. "It was you," God, that lifted me when I down, healed me when I was sick, found me when I was lost, and saved me although I deserved death! You gave me spiritual gifts assist me, and others on this journey to give you all the glory. You gave me artistic talents that help me survive, and lift your name on high by creatively sowing seeds so that others may experience you in a different way. You've also given me health and wealth, spiritually, physically, and mentally. I could go on forever speaking your praises Lord, because you are everything God and everything is you! That is the message this love letter is supposed to relay. One of gratitude, compassion, and understanding of love, I'm very grateful for the forms of love that I've been given, I reciprocate this love with compassion for those who extend it to me, and I understand the responsibility that comes with this love. Tomorrow isn't promised and anything can happen, so if for some reason I'm unable to see you or speak to you, you can play this song and be reminded of our love, who I was, and what I stood for! There has been many times during the ministering of this song that people have literally broke down in tears, including my own daughter, and myself. I'm not sure what it is about this song that makes others so emotional, but I do know for me it was the process of the transition, along with the pain required to receive the level of understanding that produced the anointing. This was the thought process and storyline behind the concept of, "It was you."

When you look at your current position and status in life, would you say that you're successful or failing? If you consider yourself successful, who do you attribute your success to? If you're failing, who do you blame or hold responsible for your misfortune? Remember that your perspective and expectancy plays a major role in your life's overall outcome. If you awake every morning with a bad attitude and a negative perspective on life, you will carry that energy around with you everywhere you go, and randomly throughout the day you'll send massive bursts of that energy into the atmosphere. As the world revolves, the law of karma or the law of reaping and sowing takes over and this just means that whatever you put out into the universe, will return to you. If you feel like you're failing in life or receiving way more bad then good, one of the first things you should check is your attitude and what type of energy you're sending into the cosmos. Most of the time, these traits are inherited by, the foundations of your upbringing, the fragility of your current situation, but mostly by the people you admire and spend the most time with. Generally, our conversations, concerns, and compassions that we share with the people in our inner circles construct our current outlook on life, and this outlook is where the bulk of our attitude comes from. With that understanding, in order to change your current undesired position, the next step requires that you come to grips with reality and accept the fact that only God can change people. Quit trying to convince yourself to believe that by investing all of your time, energy, and passion into someone, they'll become who you want them to be or the person that you see deep inside of them. Once again, only God can change people so my advice to you would be focus on getting yourself together and stop wasting valuable time. By no means am I implying that you should give up on anyone, especially, not someone that you love! However, I am saying that if you're unhappy or consider yourself to be stuck in an unfavorable position, then something has to change and since you can't change anybody else, your best option is to change YOU!

One of the biggest lies I've ever told, had the most repercussions on myself, and this was when I said, "I'll never change!" Coming up in the hood, you're taught an alternate system from what the average American learns, and you're raised with a different set of principles and values. The mentality of I'll never change, came from the sacred code of the streets, in the Keeping Real section. It is the beliefs of this culture that you must stay the same person that they've always known and loved. If not, it is considered disrespectful to your people and a violation of the code. In violation of this code, it is interpreted that you're not 'real', and the penalty could result in violence, pilferage, or total alienation from your people. The problem that I have with this section, along with many other parts of the sacred code itself, is it's a complete fallacy! It is an oppressive form of control that is marketing and adopted specifically amongst our people. Created to perpetuate self-hate and designed for us to embrace negativity and self destruction as a cool, popular trend. Please learn to stand and think for yourselves. Never accept any information from an outside source as fact without questioning, researching, and challenging both the information and the messenger. This includes but is not limited to your entertainment, education, and religion. There is no one who is able to pour into your life that should be exempt from this rule. I wasted many years of my life, attempting to uphold the rule of keeping it real and staying the same. If nothing else I learned that it is an impossible task to complete, especially if you plan on living a long life. The world is constantly evolving and changing everything in it during the process, so we must learn to embrace change because it's a mandatory part of life. It is impossible to stay the same, function, and succeed in this vastly ever-changing world that we live in today. Stop pointing, passing the buck, and blaming everybody else for your short comings. Discard the dead weight of fake friends, dream killing family members, and false prophets. Look deep within yourself to find out who you are and what you need to change in order to get where you need to be.

I learned all of these life lessons through trial and error, while conducting the process of elimination during a dark period in my ministry and life. A couple of years ago I went through a period where I was seriously unhappy. It seemed that no matter what I had accomplished or what my loved ones attempted to do for me, I couldn't shake this void of emptiness within my soul. For most people who've experienced a period like this in their life, probably would say that it was before salvation and having a relationship with Christ. It was different for me because I was saved, married, ministering, and had what I'd like to believe was a strong personal relationship with Christ. Some of you may be thinking that it's not possible but, I'd have to say that I was saved and lost at the same time! Not possible huh? Well, I didn't think so neither until I experienced for myself. Ministering through song and word for whomever, whenever they needed, but out of my gift and the obligation I felt to play 'god' for people. When I knew that you should only minister out of the unction of the Holy Spirit and with the anointing of the Lord. I wasn't doing the necessary things to replenish myself, like studying the word, attending service, or praying on a consistent basis. Therefore, I became spiritually drained but my pride had created a God complex within me that couldn't turn down an obligation to speak, show off my gifts, help someone else and/or admit that I needed help myself. This became such a problem that once my well ran dry I would just operate out of routine and what I thought would work. This kept me a float for a while, but whenever I started sinking again I wound up reverting back to the vices I gravitated to before salvation. At that point I became a straight up hypocrite, not because I was sinning, but because I was trying to change people without having a desire to change myself. It was then that I realized the difference between what I call, 'real' and 'fake' followers of Christ. The believers that I consider fake are the people who know they're imperfect but act as if they're perfect, so other imperfect people will believe they're perfect. The believers that I consider real are the ones who know they're imperfect and don't care who else knows they're imperfect because they understand that we're all imperfect in need of a perfect God!

These days I encounter so many different church houses and ministries, only to see so many ministers and leaders, in a similar position to mine during that dark period. Pastors and leaders, who are ashamed to be transparent with the rest of the congregation, because they must be viewed as the standard to follow, or at least revered above the very people they're serving. Afraid that someone is going to find out the imperfections of their character and expose their humanity, regardless of the god-like self-image they wish to sell people. There are places where people are dying and going to hell, because they can't get a word that meets them where they're at and shows them Christ. There are spiritual leaders who are more concerned with prestige, politics, and paper (money) then the omnipotent power of God and preaching his word. Delivering watered down sermons full of spiritual clichés, confusing the people with misquoted scripture, applied out of context, preaching without the anointing of God and in some cases operating in sects and cults utilizing black magic. There is so much going wrong in the world and in the church, at that time I wasn't sure that I could handle the pressure. I'm supposed to be saved, a warrior for Christ but felt like a superhero without the will to fight. I became depressed, hopeless, and stagnant. Looking at everything we were up against, including the fact that I was trying to bring a fresh breeze into the ministry and was fighting against what I considered my own people, I almost threw in the towel! It was beginning to seem like it all was pointless and the battle that I was committed to fight was a lost cause.

I remember the pain, guilt, and worthlessness that I felt as I cried before God begging that he forgive me and allow me to quit. I just felt I had taken all I could!

My intermediate family couldn't accept the transition of who I was becoming, because they couldn't get past who I was, and always had been to them. Personally, I was my worst enemy because I didn't believe in myself, nor that I could become what God was saying I already was in him. What made it even harder to accept was the fact that financially my household was suffering, as the man of the house I was being pulled in all directions and had everything riding on a ministry that wasn't working. Dealing with the streets and their reluctance to receive me because of the church boy tag that had been placed on my ministry, yet I had to face the reality of youth after youth whom I was connected to, dying and going to prison. Plus the fact that many churches and Christian brethren weren't supporting or seeding into my ministry and the disrespect I had to accept from them due to their lack of faith and understanding. For the most part I was able to turn the other cheek, but I had finally reached my breaking point and could no longer just roll with the punches. The knockout blow was received by a Christian Rap group that I was a part of called, The Coalition. The Coalition was a combination of about 10 different artistic ministries that would come together, labor and support each other no matter what. However, I was attempting to do some new and innovative things with my ministry, so I was released from the coalition and accused of 'selling-out' because they didn't understand the vision that God gave me. That was the knockout blow that left me begging for God to throw in the towel. I'm grateful that God never gave up on me, nor did he allow me to give up on myself. Instead, he dispersed angels on my behalf that would randomly appear at pivotal points in my life, when I needed someone. "It Was You," acknowledges first and foremost that it was God the whole time, and without him none of this would ever be possible. However, God also uses people to accomplish his will within the Earth, so as it relates to what we've been able to accomplish through the ministry of SaMajesty Starr. "It was you," because all this wouldn't have been possible without mighty men like Andre Barnes, Robert Gray, Marcus Seymour, Eric Hall, Mike Moore, Eric Burden, and Mike Silver. Along with the assistance from amazing women such as Karen Rawlings, Anna Hinton, Nisha Jamison, Vikki Payne, and Qwannie. Also, all of the powerful marital unions that swooped in like the Gray's, the Frazier's, the Moore's, the Morton's, the James, the Frey's, the Bussey's, the Van Irvin's and the O'Bannon's. Actually these are just a few of the angels that were sent by God to assist in this revolutionary movement, and I can't name everyone so if I forgot you then put your name in the blank "It was _____." This thing has gotten so huge and it continues to grow, but it definitely wouldn't have been possible without the support and assistance of my wife's family and my family who has sacrificed a lot to see us prosper. "It was _____" who taught, nurtured, encouraged, disciplined, assisted, interceded, sacrificed, kept it real but supported, and most of all loved us through this whole process and still continue to do so. We are eternally grateful and will forever be indebted to you.

Chapter 5 "My Legacy"

When I was a youngster and people would ask me, "What did I want to be when I grew up?" I never could answer the question because back then I couldn't picture myself as an elder. For some reason I always thought that I would die young. I had been to so many youthful home going ceremonies and was told by so many of my elders and peers that I wouldn't live to see the age of twenty-one. Not only did I begin to believe that lie but I lived like it and would speak it over myself. Until the concept of having a future and leaving a legacy became obsolete in my mind. It wasn't until I crossed that age milestone of twenty-one and had my first child (Justus Amore') that I thought, maybe there is more written for me in the book of life. It took a couple of years after that thought to realize I had a legacy and it was going to be one of power, perseverance, and triumph.

I remember sitting in the funeral service of my nieces' (Nayshauna Stoner) father Nayshaun Stoner. Who was family to me, although he and my sister (Sharleeka Clayton) never jumped the broom, In my personal opinion he was a great father with a huge heart, whom just so happened to have the street life embedded in his genetic makeup and that caused him to pass early. While ministering the eulogy the officiator Andre C. Barnes asked all in attendance this question, "What is your legacy?" Then he went on to say that you should start living each day like, you know one day you're going to die and you want people to have good things to say about you… It was at that moment when I began to become more conscious and proactive about what I was depositing into the Earth. I began to understand that I can't erase my past, no matter how much I wanted some of the events of my life to be forgotten and wished some of the mistakes I made had never happened. There was no reset button, no going backwards. What was done was done, I could only move forward from this point, attempting to stack more positivity, on top of the negativity of my past and hope that in the end my good would outweigh my bad. At that time I didn't understand that both the good and the bad worked together for the glory of those who love the Lord. Nor did I know that other people could be healed by the power of my testimony. Therefore sharing the story of what I'd been through wasn't an option because I was ashamed. There was this immense load of guilt that I carried around all the time, attached to me like a gigantic ball and chain while I did manual/ spiritual labor in the ministry. Now that I've grown and matured in my spirituality and manhood, I'm free! I'm released from the guilt and shame of my past pains and faults. I no longer drag that ball and chain around with me anymore because the Lord has broke the very chains that kept me in bondage. For whom the Lord has set free is free indeed and now as a warrior who's also a survivor, I wear my past on my chest like a badge of honor. Realizing that this is a part of my legacy and by being honest enough to become transparent before the people it enhances my life, ministry, legacy, and salvation. So I have no problem testifying about where I've been and how far the Lord our God has brought me from.

For example, there was a point in my life where I was roguish and stole so much my own mother gave me the nickname Klypto. (Kleptomaniac) This would later become my alter ego, alias and musical stage name while performing street rap. One time as a pre-teen my big sister (Sharleeka Litton) and I accompanied my mother (Sherry Threat) to the grocery store. Before entering the store I told my sister I was going to steal something. She pointed to a huge sign in the store window that said, 'Camera's are recording and shoplifters will be prosecuted!' I looked at her and said, "I don't care, I'm going to steal something anyway!" While my mother shopped for groceries that she always worked so hard to provide for us, I was sliding Butterfinger candy bars that were 3 for $1 at that time, up my Georgetown Hoyas starter coat sleeve. The crazy thing was I probably had about $5 in my pocket. I just wanted to steal something because I had a problem, however at this stage in my life neither I nor my family actually knew that I had a problem with stealing yet. Especially my mother who was pissed when the store manager told her that he believed I was stealing. She couldn't believe that he had the audacity to even assume that her son would be in the store stealing. She had one hand on her hip, the other was frantically waving her pointer finger in his face, and while her neck was rolling she was yelling, "Every time a black person enters your establishment, don't mean they are stealing. I work too hard for my money to be followed around the store when I shop and accused of theft!" As she went on, the manager was so embarrassed he became apologetic and tried to walk away but my mother wasn't finished. She was enraged, embarrassed, and wanted to prove him wrong so she told me to remove my coat in his presence. I was shocked, nervous, and scared all at the same time. My first reply to this statement was the typical, huh? You want me to do what? She said it again, take your coat off! I knew if she had to repeat herself again especially in such a heated moment I would be in serious trouble, so I prepared to be busted as I slowly slid my coat off. Somehow with about 4 to 6 candy bars in each sleeve, I slid it off and dropped the coat in the middle of the grocery store aisle. The manager was so embarrassed and apologetic he was offering mama all kinds of discounts and free merchandise. I'm still standing here in silence, mouth wide open incapacitated with amazement staring at my product filled coat on the floor. I couldn't believe that I wasn't caught red-handed. I was thinking, "It must be a miracle that I'm not a victim of child abuse or on my way to jail right now!"

Ironically, just as I began to exhale, thinking I'm home free, my mother was under the impression that we'd been stereotyped and wrongfully accused. So, she's verbally attacking the store manager.

"I don't want anything from this racist ass store, matter-of-fact; I'm putting all of my groceries back and spending my money elsewhere." Simultaneously reaching down to pick up my coat she said, "Here, Boy, put your coat on!" She grabbed the hood of my coat, snatched it up from the floor, and candy bars ejected from the sleeves like a jackpot slot machine! That was the first time I truly embarrassed my mother to the point where she cried, publicly. However, little did we know, in the future to come, there would be many other occasions where I would do something immoral or illegal to shame my family and myself.

There was another occasion, when I went to work with my grandmother, my mother's mother (Sona Clayton) because I wanted some money, but I needed to learn the value of it and the principles of labor. We performed various odd/janitorial jobs around this well-to-do, middle aged, Caucasian lady's house that in my opinion resembled Kathy Lee. I tried to just follow suit by just obeying the instructions of my grandmother however, images replayed in my head of the movie "Roots" along with other racial experiences in America on both a National and personal scale. It wasn't just the fact that she was white and we were black. It was more about the way she addressed and handled us. I think I was more infuriated because my grandmother came from a time period were this type of submission was mandatory so it didn't bother her, but I was coming from a generation of fearless, thug-life screaming rebels who were tired of asking politely and being rejected so we just took whatever we wanted. That day before my grandmother and I left her property, I stole about two-hundred dollars out of her purse and stuffed it down in the inside of one my shoes. There was no conversation about any accusations of theft made before we returned to my house so I thought I had gotten away with the crime. Only to walk through the front door of the house and hear my mother say, "Give me those filthy shoes, I just started washing a load of clothes that I need to add them to." Stunned in disbelief, I tried every excuse I could think of, just to get a moment of seclusion so I could retrieve the money before giving her the shoes, but even my animated enactment of having a bathroom emergency ended abruptly with mama saying, "Just kick your shoes off and go to the bathroom then!" Leaving me no solo space or other options but to kick the shoes off right then and there. I kicked the shoes off and started to cringe, tightening every muscle in my body as I prepared for disciplinary impact. All I received was a subtle laugh, a look of confusion, and a sarcastic comment of "Boy, something is really wrong with you!" Due to the period of time that the money was kept in my shoe, the heat from the perspiration had glued the paper to the inner toe of my shoe, and therefore I wouldn't be caught at that moment. However I was never given an opportunity to get to the washer without mama around, so when the washer stopped as she prepared to transfer that load to the dryer, she lifted the top of the washer and begin screaming my name because there was soaked twenty-dollar bills all throughout the washer. This was probably the only time in my past where I was caught stealing something and didn't receive any form of physical reprimanding. Just a long cold stare and head shaking of utter disappointment. That was the day I felt my family gave up on me, accepted I was a thief and probably wouldn't amount to much if I lived. After disrespecting my mother to the point where I disrespected her mother, that was the day I given the new nickname Klypto. The crazy thing is I would've preferred the whooping over being forced to apologize and return the money. Needless to say I had the trust of a crack-fiend amongst the entire family because everyone knew I stole and didn't have much consideration or regard for who I stole from. I can't count how many spankings, punches, and punishments I took for stealing but it didn't' matter because I would just do it again, and I didn't stop until I just personally was tired of it and found a new crime/sin to consistently commit.

Like most impoverished young black males, I smoked plenty of marijuana and sold drugs, however I took it a step further. I started robbing other drug dealers because I knew they couldn't call the police. In the worst case scenario, I would bump into one of these guys on the streets at a later date and have a shoot out for my life. I was taught the art of jacking by an O.G. (original gangster) named J-1, who before his death was feared and revered throughout Da' City as a stick-up kid/shooter. That's why when I jacked people I would do it bare faced and most times either strike them with the pistol or put it in their mouth. I wanted them to have a near to death experience, know who gave it to them, and remember me as someone who would kill or die if they came back in retaliation. Plus considering that I didn't see myself living to make the age of twenty-one, I made myself believe that I had no fear of death. The turning point came when my band of misfits and I began robbing businesses. This proved to be one of the worst choices I've ever made in my life. However before this decision was made, I was a part of an entertainment company called P.G.L. (Pimps Gangsters, and Legends) that consisted of a record company called "Winner Take All." I was the only solo artist on this indie Rap label ran by a suspected mob boss named the Black Godfather (Robert Hayes). He was rumored to be a self-made millionaire who never worked a job. In the few years we ran together he became more than my boss, he was my friend and mentor so what he was financially worth never was any of my concern. On his label I wrote and produced music for him and various other artist. I also completed my first professional solo album entitled "God Understand Me!" This was in the late 1990's, while I was still a teenager in high school. The record label made provisions for me to have my own living quarters, studio, car, album, and money. Being young, immature, and arrogant this produced a monster because couldn't nobody tell me anything. In my mind I was a ghetto superstar that was on his way to International celebrity status. During this period I shared the studio and stage with artist that included but not limited to; L.L. Cool J., Jon B., Domino, Scarface, Master P., Mystikal, Eightball & MJG etc. I was a hood celebrity where I'm from and everyone knew that disrespect or violation of me and mines could've meant death. Due to the fact that Kentucky is a Commonwealth state with no statute of limitations, I'm not at liberty to elaborate on that statement nor give any witnessed accounts, however what I will say is...It all came crashing down my senior year as God father took a trip out to the West coast to acquire a distribution deal, which he received. Yet he was unsatisfied, so he returned to the city saying he was going to film a major motion picture loosely based on his life. Although I completely disagreed with this decision because it was his money and I was his subordinate I felt I had no choice but to voice my honest opinion and be submissive. I was disappointed because I knew the "God Understand Me" album that I'd spent the past year working on, wouldn't be receiving the same distribution package he was offered on the West Coast. Instead, my project and I would now be put on the company's back burner because the main focus would be this new theatrical production.

Despite my personal feelings, I supported him the best I could in his change of direction and new strategy for the company. As the widely anticipated hood movie with a million-dollar budget movie was completed, released and nationally aired on Black Entertainment Television. The Black Godfather was arrested and federally arraigned on a host of charges including under minding organized crime, racketeering, counterfeiting, as well as conspiracy to both murder and drug charges. Word on the street was federal agents auditioned for parts, and received roles in the movie. Then they used the script and storyline claiming it to be based on his actual life events to bring charges against him. Before the night he was taken into custody, the Godfather and I met up and spoke candidly on a couple of occasions. Our topics of discussion varied but what amazed me was his poised disposition, maintaining his composure, despite the fact he was facing life imprisonment and the possibility of losing everything that meant anything to him. Regardless of what the media and judicial system says about this man, he was someone that did everything he could to help me succeed. He also saved my life more than once in the streets of Louisville and I loved him. I never told him that however these were the thoughts in my mind as we conversed and kicked it like the day of American judgment wasn't in the nearby future. We continued doing what we did best which was making music and never knew this would be the last song we would make together for at least twenty years. The studio was raided that night with the purpose of apprehending the Godfather and taking him into state custody until his federal trial began two years later. I spoke with him throughout the process, and by his own account due to the testimonies of his so-called partners he had no choice but to plead guilty. This was an action that caused him to receive over 20 years in a federal penitentiary. One by one I watched most of my hood family (his associates) be hauled off to Federal institutions and with them with the company I labored so diligently for, along with every musical work of art I produced in that time frame. I felt like a king fallen from grace and demoted to a commoner as I retuned back to the old habits and ways I lived before my iconic rise. In one day I went from hood celebrity status, on way to becoming an international star, being able to go wherever I wanted, and get or do whatever I pleased. To just another young brother on the block with mad lyrics, hustling and doing whatever he can to get by. This is when I made some of the worst decisions of my entire life!

    I began by robbing street hustlers and eventually moved up to corner stores and businesses. The next year I was booked and arraigned on charges of Robbery 1 and Complicity to commit Robbery of a business. Now I would be lying if I said I had nothing to do with this robbery. Yet I was telling the truth when I said, "This one I actually didn't commit!" However, I knew who did! I had a part in the planning knowing or unknowingly, and I was at the scene of the crime when it took place. Under Jefferson County jurisdiction laws there was no denying the complicity. That wasn't the reason I plead guilty though. I plead guilty because the so called 'G-Code' worked against me and my so called 'Ride-or-die' clique chose to ride on and let me die! When the heat was on and everybody was facing penitentiary time, fear set in their hearts, and they left me holding the bag. The prosecutor and detective just wanted a conviction, they didn't care who took the rap. The victim just wanted to cover her butt because she was getting high on the job and not following proper protocol, and everybody else involved just wanted not to be involved. Legally my lawyer and I devised a defense that was air-tight. The problem was it would require the aid of the same ones who aided in the felony offense. Even though the robber acted on his own, and the only crime we committed was not leaving him there or turning him in. The defense my lawyer had set up would release us all of any wrong doing and even create a lane for the two original snitches who called my name to recant, retract, and be released also.

After my family put up all the money that it took to fight this case for about two years, finally my defense had a break through towards the end, he told me all I had to do was subpoena the clique to attend the next trial date, and he would brief them on the strategy. Not only did I have too much faith in my team but the 'G-Code' said I couldn't subpoena my dudes! Against the advice of my counsel I took the verbal commitment of my guys that they would be there, and on the date of my trial when I was facing ten years of my life in the state penitentiary, I stood alone!

Frantically I called the homes and cell phones of my partners praying that maybe they just were running behind. Reality set in after one of the two answered his phone, and his tone along with his spoken phrase will forever echo in my head, "Uh...I'm sorry man, uh... I can't make it." I said what you mean you can't make it? And he replied "I'm scared!" Everything in me just dropped, as I stood outside the courtroom on a pay phone knowing my life was about to change forever. I thought of all the times I was scared but put it all on the line for the clique. I thought of every gang fight, street shootout, robbery, and female we shared. Most importantly I thought of every time my lawyer said, "Subpoena them." Every gangster who loved me from STL to ATL who used the phrase "No witness, no crime." They wanted to catch a greyhound to Louisville, kill the witnesses on my case, and go back home. I had been a part of this type of mafia-style favor for a favor exchange before. However, these two guys I loved like family, and we had been through way too much together. So, murder was out of the question. This battle I would have to fight alone and pray that it didn't kill me, but make me a better man. The ending result was I plead guilty to the charge of complicity and received my first felony which came with five years of probation. This is where the whole positive side of my legacy began and the SaMajesty character, that you know, was birthed.

But the first couple of years that I was on probation, I invested in the exploitations of the sex trade. Probably the biggest memory from this season of my life was renting vans and taking road trips with strippers to dance at various clubs within the region. It seemed to be very easy to find a lost, poverty stricken, ghetto struggling, single mother who felt she had nothing to lose because she was selling herself for free or for cheap anyway. By the same token it was just as simple to connect with struggling college girls, in need of tuition money, and living expenses who were wild and loved to party. In most cases they would tell me themselves, "I've done worst for too many free drinks at the bar!" By befriending them, accepting the flaws that their boyfriends and families wouldn't, while building them up mentally and emotionally, showing them my flaws, and including them in a cleverly orchestrated scheme, that we all could benefit from almost instantly. They were down with it! I never once had to steal from, beat, or force a female to do anything. We set goals and limitations in the beginning. So, I knew who was more inclined to do what and who not to include in certain things. I made a lot of money.

When someone I really cared got involved in the lifestyle, because she felt that was the only way to please me, and I couldn't get her to stop. I knew it was time for a lifestyle change, due to the fact I was too emotionally involved. I wanted to start over and knew Jesus Christ was the only way.

Regardless of what anyone thinks of me, I'm honored to worship the God I serve, who was merciful enough to save me from myself, love me in spite of me, and still make me what I'm becoming. I give all glory to God and credit part of the ministry's success to the understanding that I've been graced to be where I am, and with all the struggles I've faced, I can't see myself sitting in a seat of judgment of others. Therefore when I minister or create music, I try to keep in mind that everyone has struggles, sins, pain, and a story. If I can just remember mine and keep it in my heart. It makes it so much easier to relate and minister to others. The evidence can always be found in my legacy because of all the negative choices I've made. I stand before you now a happily married man of over five years.

My beautiful, gracious, and anointed wife (Cherrie) doubles as my best friend and business partner in the ministry. We collectively have 3 amazing children in a loving and understanding blended family. We've ministered at hundreds of churches across America in all denominational congregations. We've done countless outreaches, workshops, and community events. We've been interviewed and had music aired on Hip-hip, R&B, Country, Gospel, and University Radio stations.

We've worked with different newspaper and television stations, including my own show on Public Access Television. One of the biggest blessings is that I've had the opportunity to perform with, and for various people from all walks of life. These are just a few accomplishments made in our endeavors to assist the clergy, businesses and charitable organizations. I witnessed the power of God and the feeling of redemption after receiving a proclamation in the same city I received my felony conviction Louisville, KY.

My wife and I share the Proclamation of February 10th presented to us by the Hon. Mayor Greg Fischer. Coming from where I come from, nobody, including myself could have seen this happening. If you ask me, none of these awards or accomplishments mean as much as the family members, friends, and strangers who we impacted or helped find their way through this twisted maze called life. At the end of the day that's what's most important and that's what I want my legacy to be:

Sammy "SaMajesty" Vaughn. "He came from the darkness, to the light, and tried to illuminate the world by shinning his light wherever there was darkness!"

Chapter 6 "It's Ya Birthday"

Along this path that I've been walking for quite some time now, I've had the privilege of meeting and bonding with many people from different cultures and walks of life. I found it very interesting to learn that in some African nations ceremonies are held for groups of children instead of individual birthdays. Upon reaching a certain age in these ceremonies children are required to learn the laws, beliefs, customs, songs, and dances of their tribes. I thought that was different until my Canadian buddy told me that in Atlantic Canada, the nose of the birthday child is greased with butter for good luck. In this ritual it is believed that it makes the child too slippery for ill-luck to catch them. My friend then told me that in Quebec, they have a ritual that's similar to one we have in American ghettos. The one whose birthday it is receives a punch for each year they've lived and then an extra one for good luck! Out of everyone that I had encountered I found no custom more shocking then the Vietnamese celebration of Tet. Tet is only the beginning of the New Year, but it also means everyone's birthday. The Vietnamese do not acknowledge the exact day they were born. Everyone turns a year older on Tet, and children receive red envelopes from elder family and friends containing lucky money, called Li Xi. This was an important topic for me to have on my album for many reasons. While driving to work one morning listening to the Russ Par morning show, before they did the Zodiac jokes they were having a conversation about good and bad birthdays. Most of the sentiments people shared about what made the birthday good or bad had a whole lot to do with what kind of gifts they'd received. Not knowing that this concept of celebration would later become a song on my album, I sat in deep contemplation introspectively remembering every birthday I had or ever been a part of and this one thought connected a train of memories that ultimately took me back to the beginning.

I was born November the first in the year of nineteen-hundred and eighty. My parents have always done an exceptional job as it relates to celebrating birthdays in our family. My biological father divorced from my mother when I was about eight years of age. My mother later would marry her then boyfriend whom she's still with today Cedric Threat, whom from the very beginning I accepted and shortly after bonding with began to acknowledge as my daddy. Neither Cedric nor my mother has ever forgotten or missed an opportunity to share in the celebration date of my birth. However as far back as I can remember birthdays and holidays have always been burden filled deeply depressing days for me. I used to think that the reason for my sadness was mostly in part to my father (Sammy Vaughn Jr.) not being present, and on some occasions seeming as he even forgot it was my birthday showing up or calling days later. However because of the incident that happened to my father we always excused him from any wrong doing, pain, or inconvenience that he may have caused us. In other words my father could do no wrong.

For those who don't know my father joined the military after the birth of my big sister Sharleeka who is one year older than I am. So by the time I was born our parents were married and my father was actively enlisted in the United States military branch of the Army. By the time I was nine years of age my parents were divorced, by force of the same military branch that my father served. This is the story I was told later in life, as I matured and my family deemed me capable of handling, and I will relay this information verbatim, as I received it to the best of my ability. This event was described by my family as the breaking point. First, I was told a few stories about my manic depressive father, who had on more than one occasion put his family and himself in life-threatening situations.

However none were as devastating as the breaking point, which happened one evening after my father returned home to us from military duty. He was depressed and down in his countenance because he had received word from his superior that he was going to be stationed overseas for a couple years. Being shipped or stationed overseas wasn't foreign to my father because, in my toddler years my father was stationed in Germany, I remember because we were with him, and I think that was the major difference this time because he would be alone…we couldn't go with him! In all honesty, I'm not one-hundred percent sure, this was the determining factor of the events that was about to take place, but I do believe it had a major bearing on his frame of mind and train of thought. I can confidently say this because in retrospect, because I don't believe my father was ever a natural soldier. Before you judge me on that last statement, please allow me to explain. When I say a natural soldier I mean a true fighter, a diehard patriot with super hero aspirations who feels obligated to protect this great nation of ours. That may have been his father, or my grandfather's spirit however that was not my father's genetic makeup at all. I read into this scenario as my father was one of many young black males of his time who fell in love with a beautiful young lady, engaged in pre-marital sexual activity and became a father before he was ready or mature enough to understand what it actually meant. In order to provide for his new family and put food on the table, the quick fix answer back then was to join the military and reap the benefits of being a soldier, so that his family would be taken care of. He probably thought, "It can't be that bad, my father was a soldier his whole life and he was successful!" However he found out later in his life that he was not his father, and although his father was a soldier boy and loved it, he couldn't handle it the pressure! Because he couldn't handle the pressure, in my earlier years he would always look at me and say. "Son, when I look at you, I see myself and an opportunity to redo the many mistakes I made in my life. Don't have kids before you graduate and never enlist in the white man's military!"

{Side note: Remember that just because something works for someone close to you, doesn't mean it will work for you. What God has for you, is just for you and if you settle for anything less, you'll probably live a regretful, unsatisfying, and/or an unfulfilled life.}

I understood how he could see himself while looking at me, because often random people would say I looked like my father or reminded them of him. Another reason for that probably was because my father also had a deep passion for music embedded in his soul. He started in his youth as a singer and before he became married with kids he spent a lot of his personal time moonlighting as a club/recording deejay. After acquiring his new family he didn't immediately give up on his dreams, however he felt the welfare of his family was more important so he joined the Army military branch of service and decided to deejay in his leisure when and where he could. It is my personal belief that the stress of family life, military life, in addition to the inner turmoil of never fulfilling his dreams, or taking the proper nourishing time for himself, got the best of him and began to trigger a full blown psychological meltdown. There were phases leading up to this moment that the military and my mother experienced firsthand, they did their best to encourage and motivate my father to continue pressing forward. However I don't think that either one of them had a clue that the mental state of my father had regressed so low, until this particular evening when it turned for the worst too fast. As my mother and now deceased cousin Monte that I spoke about earlier was sitting in the living room, watching television in our Army based home of North Dietz, in Fort Knox Kentucky. My father was in the kitchen talking on the phone to one of my uncles who lived in Da' City. From the outside it seemed the conversation was about venting the pains, and stresses that were presented before them each day as men trying to protect and provide for their families.

My uncle stated, "Your father spoke of his world like an airplane losing altitude, both engines down, taking a complete nose dive and preparing to crash and burn in any minute!" He said, during the process of ministering to my father and attempting to encourage him, by letting him know that if he just gave it sometime things were going to get better. It was then that all hell broke loose, without a warning or cry for help in mid-conversation, 'POW!', through the phone lines he heard the echo a gun going off! My mother and cousin rushed into the kitchen to find my father shot, bleeding, and wrapped in the telephone chord with my uncle still on the line yelling, "Sam! Sam!"

Glory-be-to-God that my father's number wasn't called that night and he survived this selfish act of ignorant violence against himself. Because I was so young that I would've never got the opportunity to know who my father was or get the story from his own personal account. Therefore my lasting impression of him would've been that he was just a weak individual, who couldn't handle the ups and downs of life, so he took the easy way out and killed himself. I'm sorry but that's not the legacy I would want to raise my children under. Nor would I want that to be the event creating a consensus amongst the masses of who/what we are as Vaughn's, because that's not in our pedigree!

That was the moment that is defined as the breaking point! When my father's declining mental state had plummeted through the bottom of crazy, and landed flat into an area of insane. There were prior situations that took place involving my sister and I, however never one of that magnitude. For that reason the United States government board of psychiatry diagnosed my father as homicidal and suicidal. Forcing my mother to divorce him and move us away from him for the well being of all parties involved. They also honorably discharged my father from the military with full benefits and a mental check. The decision was made under the pretense of an earlier accident on the job that caused some head trauma and they believed the prior head trauma was the foundation for the mental declination and the attempted suicide. In my personal opinion, I would have to disagree because the accident which caused the head trauma was self-inflicted also.

{Side Note :} By no way am I here to judge my father, I love my father and mean him no harm. I'm simply purging myself, as honestly as I can and praying that not only those who support me can get a better understanding of who I am, but I can find the answers about me that I search for within myself!

Not having my father around wasn't the worst part of the long term effects from this episode. Being that my mother rebounded fairly quickly with an awesome black man named Cedric Threat (Pap), who came around, stayed around, and is still around as her husband. While raising his two younger brothers for his mother who was in the military, stationed overseas a lot, Pap also raised my big sister and me because of his dedication to my mother. To add to the four of us which technically weren't his, he had a child support issue from a previous relationship over his only biological son who lived with his ex in Mississippi, and as time passed he fathered three more seeds with my mother Sherrissa, Cedric, and Cedell. Pap wasn't an angel though and we had many challenges to face as a family in the beginning. Most of these have dissipated over the years and some we still deal with. The first problem was Pap and my father were friends or associates and so he basically met my mother through my father. Secondly, Pap was considerably younger than my mother and even though he was extremely responsible and mature, he was in a stage of his life where he had a lot of growing to do. My mother might indulge in an alcoholic beverage socially however she's never been a drinker. No drugs or tobacco and isn't too big on parties or the nightlife. My mother has always been a hard-working, family-oriented, straight arrow who sees almost everything in black and white. Pap was an ex-gangbanger in hoods like Del Paso Heights in California, and Memphis Tennessee. I mean although Pap came off as polite, shy, and mal-mannered. He was a heavy drinking, pot-smoker, who carried two pistols religiously, sold drugs and had a serious attitude problem. As children, how our day was going to go? Depended on what was going on in the streets that day, how much alcohol and weed he consumed, and the status of his relationship with my mother. These factors would determine rather we could look forward to an average dysfunctional family day. (This meant us fighting with the neighborhood kids because we were watching ourselves and while momma was at work, Pap was wilding with is crew.) Or a crazy dysfunctional family day, where Pap was intoxicated and infuriated, momma had a personal issue with him and the kids were caught in the middle. Wrestling, fighting, breaking things around the house, and sometimes the police would have to come to our residence and straighten things out. We've had some really explosive and potentially toxic moments in my childhood and although we've all fought like cats and dogs. To my knowledge, never has any female in our family including my mother had visual cosmetic scars. Basically in all the fights I've witnessed or jumped in my family, no female has had gashes, cuts, black eyes, or swollen facial features. I mean my parents may have fought but Pap never just walked in and punched or slapped my mother. One thing is for sure though, it always seemed like days that were supposed to be joyful like holidays and birthdays typically would be crazy dysfunctional family days. No matter what was going on though my father didn't call, visit, or say much at all. I think as children we were more worried about him doing something to himself then he probably ever worried about us. My big sister didn't care about none of the drama surrounding my mother, father, or Pap she just wanted to be with her father. I think for me as a young man, I was torn and had so many other factors to deal with.

The worst part of my father's charades was fighting and raising above the mental challenges and stigma it presented for me as his seed. Even with all the love that my mother and Pap gave I still fought daily to overcome depression and the thoughts of suicide. Every time I looked in the mirror or passed someone who knew my father I was reminded of how much I looked like him. There were times when I would have uncontrollable outbursts, nightmares, attitude and behavioral problems. It was in these moments that I would be told, "You're going to end up a psycho just like your daddy!" Sometimes I would question if my sister and I was the reason for my father's meltdown? If so, then I'd question if I would ever be father or husband material? Because I used to think that I was just like my father and if it broke him down, then maybe I wasn't cut out for it neither. Questions and thoughts like these I must admit would later prove to be the absolute worst part of the entire suicide attempt of my father, and the mental/emotional attack I would experience always seemed to be heightened around my birthday and holidays. Unlike the radio listeners who called in on the Russ Parr morning show, whose sentiments about birthdays and holidays were typically predicated by what type of gifts they received. I realized my ill feelings about birthdays and holidays wasn't because we were poor, I didn't receive great gifts, nor because we didn't celebrate extravagantly with my closest friends and relatives present. It couldn't have been any of these things because I had and did all of that on these special occasions. All I knew is that I would always subconsciously and involuntarily inherit these negative feelings around certain dates and I didn't know why. I was always happy on other people's special days even though I may not have had the money or resources to shower them with lavish gifts or at least the gifts I felt they deserved. Especially as it related to the women in my life like my grandmother, mother, sisters, daughter, and wife. That would be the only downer about celebrating birthdays with them because I love them so much I always want to do something really special for them and can never afford to do so.

{Side note: As a parent, in this current generation I believe we put too much emphasis on tangible items that our children ask for, and we want them to have. Sometimes, these items take precedence over the installment of the fundamental morals and values that we were raised with. Not to downplay the impact of rewarding our loved ones with gifts to say, " Good job! I'm Proud of you! Or this is something to encourage you and let you know that I enjoy making you smile." However, the receiving of any man made products should never be confused with the meaning of true love, unless it's an engagement ring and even that ring should not be equated with love, but only serve as a symbol or representation of a promise or covenant of love!}

To this date I still don't know why I experience these ill-feelings around certain calendar days of the year. However I do know that it doesn't affect me as bad as it used to so I'm getting better. Until a couple of birthdays ago, I would spend the whole day drinking alcoholic beverages and smoking marijuana until I was too sick to function. This was an urban ghetto ritual that became a tradition due to my circumstances, surroundings, and circle of friends. What's crazy is, when I finally decided to change my life and make a commitment to live my life consistently maintaining a certain level of sobriety, I didn't know how to celebrate anymore. I had to teach myself new ways of having fun and enjoying life without self-destructing. The past few birthdays I've spent reflecting in seclusion or performing/ministering to the masses somewhere. Now, that I'm in my thirties with three children of my own it seems that celebrating my birthday becomes less important than just being grateful I was graced another year and blessed with the opportunity to watch over my seeds and witness them grow, as I continue to serve the Lord! I guess birthdays now have become a sign of aging and maturity where I'm constantly reminded where the Lord has brought me from. How he saw fit to keep me and bring me through even when I couldn't see it, because as I stated before I never thought I'd live to see twenty-one and I've surpassed thirty-one. Now, I would be lying if I said I no longer get a little depressed on my birthdays, or if I said I didn't have drink here and there from time to time. However what I can say honestly and proudly is the vices that I used to stay depressed on my birthdays I don't use anymore. I have great birthdays without being falling down drunk, or so high that I have to sleep it off! Furthermore I no longer blame my father for any decisions that he made as it relates to his life. I understand now that each one of those decisions was a part of his legacy and the alteration or deviation of any single one would have rewrote history, drastically changing his life, mine, and ultimately who and what I've become. Through repentance and forgiveness given to me by the power of my Lord and savior Jesus Christ I release my father and myself from any ill-feelings harbored over the years. Money is no longer a factor in showering my children/family with love and drugs/alcohol isn't the foundation, means, or tools for celebrating God's gift of another year on planet Earth. That's why I felt compelled by that morning radio broadcasting to create this song called, "It's Ya Birthday!" Although it's still a rough time of the year for me, I celebrate tactfully and tastefully for all the right reasons. This song helps to remind me that each birthday is very special because I'm not even supposed to be here. I no choice but to celebrate and Go Hard! For every zodiac sign represented on every birthday, may this song become an anthem for anyone who wants to bring that special day in right! "Go head, It's Ya Birthday and you better throw!"

Chapter 7 "Gimme Some Room"

Have you ever been somewhere or with someone in your life where you felt it wasn't alright to be yourself? Have you ever felt challenged in your individuality, to the point where it was uncomfortable or unnatural for you to be you? What about a time or situation where you wanted to fit in or earn a sense of belonging so bad, that you completely created or became a whole new character, for someone else's acceptance or approval? Can you recall ever having a period in your life where you didn't know who you were? Or then again maybe you did, but felt like the raw and uncut (REAL) you, wasn't good enough? If so, did you subconsciously or involuntarily began to take on an alter ego or adopt another personality/character? If you have this process is called an identity crisis, it's a horrible feeling for you not to know who you are, and a very dangerous place to be! You can trust me on this one because I know all about it! I've been through a lot of different situations in my life, forcing me to wear a lot of different hats and ultimately I've seen and learned a lot of different things. I consider myself a survivor via Jesus Christ and the application of the gift God bestowed upon me of adaptation. There are many gifts of the spirit and often we over look some of our best ones because they don't come with fame, fortune, or prestige. There's no such thing as a small gift in the spirit, each one is very important or God wouldn't have wasted time given them to us. These gifts are mandatory for survival, to fulfill our individual destinies, and to complete the purpose of our existence. In the book of Romans, Chapter 11:29 says, "the gifts and callings of the spirit are without repentance." In my own understanding this means that we were given a destiny, gifts and purpose even though God knew we would engage in sinful lifestyles that we probably wouldn't be repenting for. Yet, he chose us anyhow. He still hasn't changed his mind about us, and he will never give up on us if we don't give up on him! God doesn't make mistakes, we do! Yet regardless of how many or which ones we make, while under his covering the gift will go forth in due season and reap a harvest. This means that just because you're effective or impactful operating in your gift or calling, doesn't necessarily mean that God is pleased with you personally. In the book of Proverbs, chapter eighteen, in verse sixteen it states that your gifts will make room for you and bring you before great men. The gift can do that alone, so as the gifted or the vessel it is your sole responsibility to acquire and maintain your own salvation. Can you imagine being a vessel that creatively delivers a word from God? A word that's so powerful it finds the lost, binds with their soul, and makes them feel whole again by mending together the broken pieces of their life. A word that not only directs but literally transports them to salvation, and as the vessel who brought them, you're only allowed to watch them enter the golden gates because you've been denied access on a technicality. Believe it or not, this was the thought process behind the critically acclaimed secular song, "Gimme Some Room."

{Side Note: Music is a very powerful tool. It is so powerful that it was part of the reason Lucifer himself became so arrogant and envious of God that he had to be banished from Heaven and took a third of the angels with him. Music is so powerful that even today it is still regarded as a weapon for both sides in the spiritual warfare we face daily. Knowing the immense power of music it allows me to see the obvious importance of its application in evangelism. Now I don't and never will agree with the murderous and vulgar lyrical wordplay of devil worshipping, demonizing, soul depleting compositions. However I feel the same way about all my media choices, television and pc included not just my musical selections. I also believe that there is a line that sometimes we must walk for the sake of saving the lost! In the grand scheme of things,

that is our mission and I believe it requires one to come out of their comfort zone in order to meet people where they are. This may not be your calling or for you to even understand however be careful judging others or telling people what is and isn't of God because no human mind is capable of fully understanding the works and ways of the Lord. Just because you don't understand a move, agree with it, or see God in it doesn't mean that he isn't there! Everyone has a lane, just do your best to stay in yours and complete the mission in which he has entrusted you with.}

I have chose and been chosen to travel many different paths thus far in my life, which has afforded me the opportunity to hold many positions/titles both good and bad. Without hesitation, I would say the most difficult position I've ever maintained is that of a Christian leader in the field of urban praise. This statement may be hard for many people to accept however, it is simply my truth. I say this because for everything I may have been in the streets, rather I was accompanied by a gang or solo, I was afforded the opportunity to be my natural sin sick self. This was the character that emerged from within my subconscious, with the addition of more negative traits, and tricks that I'd randomly pick up. There's two sides to every book, so even though my natural character was dark and sinful, the positive side was being able to recognize that I have another side and therefore could pray and work on the error of my ways. I confess that although I didn't like who I was, it was still me and it's still a part of me that I have to deal with from time to time. It is in those times I scream Hallelujah and plead the blood of Jesus Christ. I'm eternally grateful for his grace and mercy through the process of saving me from me. Feeling the need to give back in an attempt to help other young lost souls, brought me to a position of leadership where I could use my gifts and talents in the ministry. I entered the church with a radical approach to witnessing and an energized spirit of urgency. Ironically after Christ saved me, it was his church that knowing or unknowingly tried to kill me and send me back to the dark place I came from. I can't exactly tell you why because I'm not completely sure, however I do know how. It was the constant preaching at me and not to me, demonstrating a lack of understanding and correlation. This ensured that I never felt a sense of belonging in the ministry, nor in our father's house. I felt like the church was similar to typical American culture, it was always something dealing with my outward appearance or character that made people feel, I wasn't welcome or worthy to be a part of the fold. Cosmetic issues like my hair, my clothes, and the ways that I wore them seemed to give the impression that I wasn't sophisticated enough. I was consistently shunned for my conversation and the usage of slang lingo or hood mannerisms, instead of biblical scriptures or spiritual cliché's. It was an obvious fact that I didn't know proper church protocol nor how and when to praise God. I've never been one to just jump on the band wagon or to say silent when I felt I was being mistreated. Therefore, I questioned a lot of things other members seemed scared to challenge and was always vocal about something that didn't make sense or seemed unfair. This created a lot of discontentment in the hierarchy of the upper ranks and frustration amongst the officers of the order. Above all I personally believe that I intimidated many of them, mostly by having a true but harsh testimony that I wasn't ashamed to share because it seemed honesty about where you came from or what you was still battling was strictly prohibited.

    I am one-hundred percent man, strong, genuine and only fearful to God. It is my belief that because the modern church of today is so feminine and submissive this made many members as well as leaders afraid or uncomfortable in my presence. It seemed their response to ease the tension or build their own self-confidence was to make me a clone of them or just tell me I didn't belong. They figured if I felt I really belonged there and wanted to stay then, I would take note of the list of things I needed to change about me in order to be saved or fit in and comply. Being as I was a fresh face in the ministry and a baby in my faith I thought maybe they were right. I remember thinking to myself, who am I? These are spiritual veterans and who would know more about Christ and what he desires then them. Without doing any research, praying, or seeking God on the matter because I didn't know I should've at that time. I began trying to reshape my character in an effort to please the powers that be. In retrospect, I find it funny that as filthy as I was when God found me and brought me out, I was good enough for him to call and use. Yet even after washing up, I still wasn't good enough for his people and I never thought something seemed strange about that.

While working on my, to do list, 'becoming a real Christian'. I received a vision from the Lord that detailed his purpose for me and the calling on my life into the ministry. This vision complicated things for me because it seemed to contradict what the saints and church leaders had just told me I needed to do. In this vision I was a modern day David who's years in the fields (streets) as a hustler, gatherer, herder (hustler/leader/protector). Put me in situations where I battled wild beasts (thugs/the system) for my life. During this training period I spent plenty of alone time with the Lord which created a major trust (faith) and worship (urban praise) in me. This would later (now) bring me before the king (leaders), to fight (revolt) against Goliath (tradition) on behalf of the nation (church). By defeating Goliath I would liberate (unify) the saints and bring victory (salvation) to all of Israel (the lost/current generation). Not by confidence in myself but faith in the almighty God I serve, I knew this goal could be accomplished however I couldn't use the kings armor (the traditional methods his whole army was using). In order to defeat Goliath I had to come a new way, my own style of fighting that I was comfortable with and had worked for me many times in the past. I just needed my sling (music) and some smooth stones from the freshwater brook (lyrics covered in the anointing of the living word). Just like David I had been in the fields so long that my own family overlooked me so when the prophet anointed me as the one, no one believed it and I wasn't sure what to do so I went back to laboring in the fields doing what I'd always done. When the time came for battle I was without fear of the enemy because I figure after all God has brought me through in the fields surely I won't die here! However because the king requested, I tried on his armor and realized that this is what everyone else has on, who looks prestigious in the kings army yet they have no intentions on fighting Goliath.

What if I told you in the midst of all the confusion and fearful talk from the king and his counterparts, what God was showing me were my own insecurities. For a brief moment I completely forgot who I was in Christ, my gifts, capabilities, and the purpose for which I was brought before the king. If God wanted it done their way then he just would've used them. That's why I still say the hardest title I've ever had to maintain is that of a leader in the ministry of urban praise. In retrospect I believe that against all odds it was just hard to view myself being and walking in what God called me to be. My vision only went as far as where I came from, what people said about me, and what I perceived they saw when they looked at me. Armed with a word from the Lord, while sharing my heart, testimony and the vision that God gave me, I still wasn't received by the leaders and elders of the church. Many of them don't see the relevance of youth ministry and typically write us off because most of us haven't been to seminary. This ministry is a major challenge these days because often the youth are in the streets dying, at the same time the churches without youth participation and presence are dying also, and in my field you stand in the gap trying to present a solution to the problem. Sometimes it feels like a winless battle because in most cases, you fight with the streets because many of them view the church as unrealistic and hypocritical. Then you fight with the churches because most of them view street people as unworthy and hell bound. What this means for your ministry is its very hard to establish a network, a following, resources and finances to keep going. It's very common that as the leader of these types of ministries you must pay for it out of your own pockets because typically those you're witnessing to either don't have the money or it's not their favorite choice of music consumption and the church your witnessing with don't really like Rap music or connect its relevance. Often they may invite you to come and help build up the youth presence or keep the youth occupied for a while however they don't want to financially sow into your ministry to do so. Most times you end up alone in gymnasiums or family life centers ministering to large groups of youth who may love your method of ministry however, they don't have money to sow into your ministry so you end up giving away product. It's a sad chain of events but when you know you're called to do it, you just have to keep believing that God will make a way, as you faithfully continue searching for other creative ways to keep your ministry going.

{Side Note: If there is someone reading this right now who is supposed to be active in the ministry but won't move forth because they feel bound by their own personal struggles. Accept this written message as a divine appointment, between the spirit of the living lord and you. None of us are perfect and will cease to be until the return of Jesus Christ. The fact that you battle with a stronghold or certain sins just validates the fact that you're human and therefore you have an obligation to help someone else because you can relate to the struggle. I'm willing to step out on faith and say the nature of your sins or the battles you fight for your own salvation, is probably going to be closely related to your purpose or calling to the ministry. I pray that the chains are broken, so that

you can be liberated and encouraged to embrace your individuality in Christ. We were all fearfully and wonderfully made different for a reason and you can never live out the full potential of your life without embracing and utilizing all of you! The attempt to be anything or anyone other than yourself is like saying you're not good enough or God's work in creating you wasn't good enough. Both of which are lies from the pits of hell, you're as close to perfect as humanly possible and the only changes you need to make is probably in the area of friends and faith.}

Now I don't mean if you're gravely obese and unhealthy so you're trying to lose a few pounds, or saving up for a mandatory corrective or constructive surgery because honestly it becomes a different conversation when we start talking about cosmetics. The message that I'm trying to get out there is your personality, talents, character, etc; are attributes that in addition to your pain will ultimately create your lane in ministry and life. However please understand this will not be an easy task considering we live in a day and age where people are uncomfortable, afraid, or ashamed to live in their own skin. These days everybody fights to be accepted in a group or just part of the crowd, and to be different means to be out casted, misunderstood and often disrespected. It's almost a cardinal sin to have your own personality, ideas, character and beliefs these days. In my personal opinion it's that same psychotic, controlling, self-righteous in arrogance attitude that's ushering in World War III and the spirit of the anti-Christ. There are many people who stand alone however most belong to groups, cells, or whole nations that believe their religion and beliefs are the only way to world peace and spiritual salvation. Somehow in their mind, culture, or religion anyone who doesn't agree or comply is considered the devil or the enemy and should be put to death. In most cases although religion and spirituality is heavily spoken of, it's hard to see the works of God in people that are so relentless with power, hateful, unforgiving, self-absorbed and merciless. When you dissect a lot of the superficial issues, looking past the lies and publicity stunts you'll be able to see the truth and capitalistic struggle for world domination. Enough is never enough and somebody has to have it all! Therefore I'm telling you that I don't know what you believe but whatever it is, stand firm on it and be willing to die for it because that just may be the ending result anyway.

"…a man without anything to fight and die for isn't fit to live!" -MLK

I finally reached a point in my life where I feel that radical about my beliefs, my calling, my family, and myself in general. I understand now that wherever I wasn't or am not accepted is because I'm not supposed to be there. Jesus, his ministry, and ministers were denied in many places also, that doesn't mean your ministry isn't needed or relevant. Nor does it mean that the ones who didn't receive it or that are attempting to kill it for lack of understanding are the devil. It simply means retune your spiritual ears and make sure you're hearing the navigational system of the Holy Spirit. Follow the steps in the order that God has given you, to complete the task in which he has entrusted you with. I was upset and frustrated with people until God convicted me in my heart and showed me this. I was only upset because I put certain people on a pedestal and held them to such high regards that I expected them to agree with me and my task. Why? These people didn't come from where I came from! These people didn't know my heart, nor could they see the vision that God gave me and what all came along with it. That's why this song is so important to me. "

"Gimme some room / …", Get thee behind me Satan! "Gimme some room / …", enlarge my territory oh God! "Gimme some room / …", grace me Lord as I step out on faith, in obedience to your word, and go boldly where no man has dared to go! As for all you haters, naysayers, and spectators just "…gimme some room / back up and let me show you what to do with it!"

This concept first struck me while attending a youth conference/praise festival called C.R.U.N.K. fest (Christ Raising up New Kids fest). This is an annual Christian event hosted each year by the awesome youth ministry of a church called New Mount Zion, in Shelbyville Ky. I have been blessed to be a part of this festival since its origin over five years ago and witness the glory of God as each year it grows in leaps and bounds with more lives being saved and forever changed. I have so much love and respect for the dynamic, anointed, union of the angels of that house pastors Cassandra and Kilen Gray. There is so much that I could say about this righteous, and beautiful covenanted couple, who are a spiritual power house and a major blessing to the body of Christ through multiple ministries. Yet I challenge you to do your diligence and research them for yourself. What I can tell you about them is, even in the beginning of my ministry when most pastors took advantage of or shunned me, these are two of the few who believed and sowed into my life every chance they got, and I pray that God blesses them in abundance for saving my marriage, ministry, and life!

While attending one of these Crunkfest events I witnessed the overwhelming response of unsaved attendance because it was held in a hotel conference room, and promoted publicly on all broadcasting stations as a family event. The most powerful piece to this puzzle was the eclectic combination of arts, entertainment and ministry. Spoken Word, Rap, contemporary gospel, skits, etc; I mean they used everything they could to draw a crowd and worship the Lord. There was even a performance of dancing that's typically outlawed in most churches or Christian venues called krumping. This is typically considered a secular dance however that night it was ministered tactfully and tastefully, with historical explanations and biblical connotations. I was a witness to so many unsaved youth who came to see Tight Eyez, who is known as one of the originators of this form of dancing. While watching him krump, these youth were ministered to and many of them gave their life to Christ with a new concept of being a Christian and using creative ways to seek and save the lost. In the midst of praying, shouting and giving God the glory I saw another vision....

There was a huge nightclub in the midst of the city that was filled with youthful souls. From the outside you just knew they were having a ball dancing and doing what they normally do as if God wasn't a factor. Surrounding the club was masses of saved folk picketing, praying, and witnessing in an attempt to detour these youth, some of which were their own from going inside the club. If the youth decided to go in this club then they were written off as demon possessed and hell bound. I myself was a part of the church crowd but had a yearning to enter the club. I remember feeling like, "if I could just get in there, I could at least save the ones who were only there because they didn't agree with the beliefs and practices of the saints outside". Most of the youth that was going in this club were also believers, who hadn't condemned themselves just yet. Like me, they knew they had a calling on their life and a place in the kingdom however felt they didn't fit or wouldn't be received so they figured why even try? In this vision I was literally begging the saints of God to grace me the opportunity to go into what they considered enemy territory and attempt to witness to them another way then what we were doing outside already. They rebuked me and warned me that if I went in, all of them along with God himself would wash their hands of me. Finally, an angel of the Lord appeared illuminating a path through the saints that parted them like the Red Sea and commanded that I go forth. I was told not look at them, beg for permission, nor even explain why I must go. My instructions were to follow the path only asking for room to walk through, do and say exactly what the spirit tells you unapologetically and watch what the Lord our God does! So I made my way through the crowd and into the club screaming Back, Back, I got the spirit with me and I'm a show you what to do with it, "Gimme some room /..."!

I wasn't allowed to see what happened when I walked into the club but I do understand the vision and why the song had to be labeled just Hip-Hop and not gospel. Regardless to how people may feel about me and my cause, I'm committed to saving the lost not the saved, and in order to reach them I must go where they're at, speaking in a language or with a tongue that they can understand. Being obedient to his word I've been in a lot of secular venues, done many secular shows/concerts, received spins and been interviewed on secular radio/television stations. In most cases labeled as an activist or just a Hip-Hop artist, however the blessing has been that so many people in other cultures or from different walks of life have been exposed to the teachings of Jesus Christ, and accepted him by being introduced to him in a different way while at the same time being accepted for who they are individually. Faith, obedience, compassion, and transparency are very big keys to the ministerial work that I do. I hope that this chapter has enlightened or encouraged you in some shape, form, or fashion to embrace yourself and walk boldly in the way that our Lord God has called you. Hopefully the next time there's a shift in the atmosphere and you're given a challenge that you know is of God and people try to stop you or slow you down. Before you fight the spirit and miss a golden opportunity, by being twisted up in an identity crisis trying to figure out if you're in his will or not. Trust the word of God and vision he gave you that others can't see. Tell the haters, naysayers, and spectators, "Gimme some room /...Back! Back! / Let me show you what to do with it!" Never apologize for being you, because that's why God made you so unique. Matter-of-fact people should apologize to you for wanting you to be anything else, and remember that God can take you anywhere, and will take you everywhere, just don't forget it was God who took you there....Exalt him!

Chapter 8 "Mrs. Perfect"

This chapter and song was written for all the single people out there who always say, "Love/Marriage just isn't for me!" For those individuals who think and act like they're God's gift to the opposite sex and there isn't one who was created that deserves all of them. The bachelor and bachelorette that views themselves as too needy and complicated for a potential suitor to please and keep satisfied. This chapter is for all of you! From the indecisive dater who has many options of relationships but can't pick one that they're willing to give a serious chance, to the hopeless romantic whose really given up on love due to lack of trust in the opposite sex. There are a thousand scenarios, philosophies, and mindsets that one can have as it relates to dating, sex, and love. Which granted is a very popular yet touchy subject and I'm not here to condemn, nor tell you what, or how to do anything because I don't know your story. I just hope that you're receptive enough to hear mine and just maybe it'll bless you.

Previously in this book I briefly spoke about some of my escapades in relationships; you would probably think for someone who has managed to accomplish and conquer most of a young man's immature fantasies, I must be pretty cocky! If that is what you assumed then you would be absolutely incorrect. Although generally throughout my entire life I've been viewed as a 'pretty boy' by others, I've never felt that level of self-confidence or even believed that I was attractive. I can't recall ever looking into a mirror and feeling good about the reflection staring back at me. I bring this up because self-confidence, self-value, and overall acceptance of self are popular human issues shared both inside and outside the church. There are way too many people in this great but vain country of America with low self-esteem and issues with self-confidence. You would be surprised how many everyday people, as well as celebrities that you may consider to be flawless that battle with these same issues. If you don't believe the importance of finding a cure for this problem, do some research on societal illnesses and see how many times one of these flaws show up on the list of symptoms. Every major wave starts and ends with a ripple. Some of the major problems we experience in this country began with a lack or misunderstood sense of self. Domestic violence, depression, drug abuse, and teenage pregnancies are just the tip of the iceberg. We always ask people how, and why'd they get caught up in these vices? I think the real question may be why is this modern day society and current generation having such a huge problem with being comfortable in their own skin?

    I'm not going to pretend as if I have all the answers, however I have been pondering on the subject and I'm prepared to offer some logical explanations for your personal review in your leisure or at your earliest convenience. I will begin by saying the media and public programming has a large part to with it. I say this because the media classifies you by where you live, how you dress, who you hang around, etc., and they sway the views and ideas of the consensus on each categorized individual. This can manipulate or determine how you feel about strangers, stereotypes, politics, profiling, etc. However more importantly though, this can ultimately mold the views and opinions about the people that you do know, and yourself! Public programming would be next in line of responsibility because it shapes your ideas and opinions on everything. The radio sings to you what makes you love, what makes you party, and what makes you horny. While the television casts images of every aspect of human life including how it is and isn't supposed to be lived. Every time you turn on the television it tells you what's beautiful and sexy reminding you of how far you are from the ideal image. We all know that sexy and beauty, both are held in the eye of the beholder, yet we spend numerous calendar days and countless hard earned dollars trying to fit an image of what society calls perfect.

I myself fell into this trap at an early age because I grew up in a time period when dark-skin people wasn't considered attractive at all. I've always been height-challenged, and weight just never stuck to my bones. Short, black, skinny and poor has never been qualities that would earn you a spot on the list of most eligible bachelors or considered in 'most desirable' conversations amongst women. The image of my kind on television or in magazines wasn't common and when portrayed it was typically in a derogatory fashion. Usually when people gave me a comment it always had a tag on it. Like, "he's cute…for a black boy"! Or "you're very handsome…to be dark-skinned!" In my mind people would just compliment me to be nice or because I carry my age well and I've always been built like a teenager. As far as my luck with the ladies, I attributed most of that to my creative talents and aspirations of being wealthy one day. It was always something about having a dream that a woman could believe in and maybe share or reap the benefits from that made her willing to overlook personal or character flaws that she normally wouldn't have. My other big advantage back then was my commitment to the thug life. That dangerous, rough neck, unpredictable, wild side was madly attractive to the young ladies back then during the Tupac Shakur era.

In retrospect, I believe that we couldn't see it because we didn't understand it but it was the anointing of God on me, even back then giving the impression that one day I would be a great man amongst men. Because sometimes there's a spiritual connection between two people whose destinies were written to interact and intersect at a certain point in life for a greater humanitarian cause, and because one or both may not know or understand their mission or purpose, this spiritual energy has the potential to become negative if channeled incorrectly at an inopportune moment. This concept was too advanced for my young mind to comprehend back then, however I totally understand it now and realize that's exactly what I was doing. Whatever it was that brought people to me, because I had a horrible sense of self I took every opportunity to exploit them for selfish gain and in the process I left a trail of broken hearts and assassinated characters behind me. Now that I'm older I realize the painful ripple effect associated with the process of long term healing from emotional scars. There are certain relationships in our lives that we invest so much more in than we realize while we're still connected to that person. It isn't until after that relationship doesn't work out and we attempt to dust ourselves off and try again, that if we're lucky we're able to see the areas that need work or rebuilding. However often there isn't any introspection, there's just the blame game and a self-gratifying justification of why we are what we have become and typically we bring this attitude and emotional baggage into the next relationship, destroying their psyche, scarring their heart and leaving them to repeat the cycle in another toxic relationship.

    I hate to admit it but I was one of those people and it took a lot of introspection, honesty, and prayer that came with a lot of pain. I'm still working on this however I'm growing stronger and getting better every day. I believe the old saying is, "Hurt people hurt people," and if you can trace your pain back to the beginning, you can locate the cause and reasons for your actions. In accordance with this philosophy tracing my pain led me to my eighth grade year in middle school. I have to start here because all throughout middle school while my peers were dating and experimenting with their sexuality I wasn't, and it wasn't because of my religion because then I didn't have one nor was it because I didn't want to because I did. My main problem was I lacked the necessary social skills required in building relationships, the reason being that I lacked a positive sense of self. In my mind regardless of the 'pretty boy' compliments that I received, I was still nappy-headed, skinny, short, black, and broke owning like three pairs of pants that I just switched shirts to daily. My self-confidence was down, I devalued myself, and my overall perception of me was negative. However without swag or a sense of fashion I gained access to the 'cool clique' late in sixth grade year because I constantly exhibited my Rap/freestyle abilities. Despite the fact that due to the limited selections of my wardrobe, I had uniforms before uniforms became mandatory in public schools, and was still considered a pretty boy who was part of the cool clique because of my extraordinary lyrical talents. Most pre-teens who have or will experience this phase of life, typically aren't so lucky because image was and still is very important in the cruel hearts and superficial minds of students in this fragile yet impressionable age group. The exception was made for me because I was known for my quick wits and creative ability to put together an impromptu rhyme about anyone, anything, anytime, and anywhere! This meant even though I was cat raggedy, I was the last person you wanted to challenge at a game of the dirty dozens. I had low self-esteem so I would lyrically chop myself down first before starting in on you and your family, creating a major scene for my peers to witness and cheer me on. To make matters worse I had a short tempered fuse, didn't mind fighting and had a group of peers that would side with me on anything because I was known as The Candy Man! Remember earlier, I told you the story about getting caught stealing butterfingers while at the store with my mother and sister. Well for the record when I typically went anywhere to steal, in most circumstances I went alone. Stealing or boosting merchandise was something that I practiced more than twice a week, because I would set-up shop in my locker and sell these products at school; The Candy Man!

    I had a creative talent and a street hustle with a low sense of self and horrible social skills. This is why I had an initial problem with dating or courting the females. The first public display of admiration I experienced, oddly enough came from a Caucasian girl named Courtney. The problem with this was my family was totally against inter-racial dating back then and constantly vocalized their feelings about it. They would make comments like:

"That's not the reason our ancestor's fought and died for!"

"If she can't use your comb then don't bring her home!"

"Alright, that jungle fever is gon' end up getting you twenty-five to life because you can't trust them, they'll set you up."

"Mark my words, those white girls aren't nothing but trouble!"

Between my family and friends I've heard every racist joke and derogatory stereotype about dating outside my race that's ever been created. The statement that always tickled me was, "You know he don't like sistahs, he like 'em other girls!"

The truth that they never knew back then was I had no social skills so I liked whoever liked me, because I lacked what it took to go after what I wanted, I often would settle for whatever came after me, and in this case it was a blonde hair, blue-eyed girl named Courtney.

{Side Note : For the record, I've never been discriminative as it relates to dating. However, after my first encounter, inter-racially, it was something about exploring the unknown and studying the differences that fascinated me. I didn't know that this was unhealthy as it related to dating and could form a habit of lustful infatuations with females outside my own, subconsciously, making you discriminate against your own kind. }

Nevertheless, here I was in Junior high school, going through puberty, and the first opportunity I received for courtship was Courtney. My mind, emotions, and most importantly my hormones were racing so I ignored the prejudice forewarnings of my inner circle and went for it. Courtney and I was a private couple, talking on the phone and sneaking around the school for private time. It was during this time that I learned what fellatio felt like, because I was too shy to kiss her one day she said, "You don't have to kiss me, I'm going to kiss you!", she started on my stomach and never kissed above it!

Our private relationship was good as long as no one at school found out about it and of course they did! My nose was so wide-open, I told everybody because I thought Courtney was my girlfriend and we were in love. After her Caucasian peers found out that she was dating a black guy, they bullied and tormented her so bad she denied our relationship and for the rest of the year ignored my existence. The silver lining of that cloud was this beautiful, nice-shaped, red-bone who was a cheerleader began this dialogue with me. Her name was Ann, and Ann's main conversation was based around trying to figure out how a brother like me could date white girls when there were so many beautiful single black girls. She thought I was conceited and had something against black girls. She never would've imagined my self-image was that low and I just accepted Courtney because she accepted me. Ann was totally disgusted by the fact that not only was I dating Courtney but to add insult to injury I let her play me like a fool! She really wanted to fight Courtney but I thought Ann was too intellectually deep and all around beautiful to be fighting, so I made her promise that she wouldn't then Ann and I became good friends.

However quiet as kept my, even though I got upgraded to Ann, I had a personal vendetta against Courtney because I was embarrassed and my feelings were hurt. I wanted her to hurt too so I devised a plan that took almost the rest of the year to complete. As a class, we were taking a trip to Chicago Illinois, because this would be our last year together before moving on to High School. I overheard her talking to her friends about how proud her parents were of her and how much shopping she was going to do in Chicago. Being as I was already a thief, I made it my personal mission to find a way to steal her purse before it was time to go on that trip. I just wanted to see her cry and I did, while spending her money frivolously in Chicago before her very eyes and she never knew. Unfortunately for me, stealing the purse was easier then stealing from the store and the curiosity of what was in different women's purses led me to a new form of theft, that seemed to be more lucrative then the previous. I started taking from or taking the whole purses of random white girls but by the time the year was out I had added a couple of black girls and even a few teachers to my list of victims. This behavior continued until eight grade graduation and no one knew anything about it.

My mother would find random school identification cards or purses in the alley out back of our house and interrogate me like a detective. To no avail because I wouldn't break and there wasn't any notification from the school about a potential threat or problem. So, she would always end the line of questioning with this evil look and say, "I know you doing something and if I ever find out what it is, I'm gon' f*** you up!" This was before the grocery store incident so my mother couldn't tie it all together yet.

Meanwhile I was feeling like I was untouchable, some type of slick, cat burglar operating as a criminal mastermind that everyone was incapable of catching. It would later take the grocery store incident with my mother and then the incident where I was caught red-handed stealing from my grandmothers employer to put an end to that type thievery, however as you've already read this problem would resurface a little later in my life on a grander scale.

As, for now I was an eighth grade graduate headed to High school in the fall and enjoying my current summer vacation with my first legitimate girlfriend, Ann. She was a beautiful, curvy, African-American cheerleader and we were happy in teenage love.

For the first time I was beginning to understand what it felt like to have confidence, I walked around like I was the big man on campus, and nothing or no one could bring me down. However I didn't understand the difference between having confidence in myself and being prideful in what I possessed. When school started in August of that year, I began my freshman year in high school under the impression that I was confident and I had to be worth something because my girl loved me and she was flawless. I was still short, skinny, black, broke, and technically a virgin who had never kissed a girl outside of my family. None of which mattered at that time, this new found confidence in myself, brought all kind of unwarranted attention from female prospects who heard I was dating a fancy cheerleader from another school.

I didn't even flinch at them or their desperate attempts to conquer the new guy and crush the illusion of love Ann and I thought we shared. At least three times a week after school I would walk or ride my BMX bicycle over to Ann's house, which was probably about two miles distance. We would talk for hours, walking or playing little games outside but most of the time I was a comedian and no matter what she was going threw I would make her laugh until it hurt. At this point we had been together for six months and I'd yet to build up the courage to take a swing at the ball, let alone run any bases.

I figured she was getting frustrated because we began to talk about sex a whole lot more and even though we hadn't even French kissed we planned to have sex in November. We chose this month because my birthday was at the beginning of November and hers was at the end. We spent hours together in person and on the phone discussing what we were going to do to each other when the time came and I played it cool even though I was so nervous I was stealing pornographic videos for lessons. I think the biggest fear for a young man is you don't want to be a disappointment, especially when it's her first time because no matter how many encounters she has throughout her life span she'll never forget her first one, and all this pressure became stressful being as I was too scared to even kiss the girl already.

Inevitably time passed and it was the weekend before her birthday. I figured the easiest way to do this would be to get her a gift for her birthday that was so special, she would be filled with excitement and couldn't resist kissing me so I wouldn't have to initiate the sex.

I was fourteen years old tops, so I needed a ride to the mall and convinced my elder cousin Eric to take me so that I could find a gift, although I had no idea of what type of gift to get her. Needless to say, we spent a couple of hours in the mall. While I was tirelessly going from store to store looking for the perfect birthday present, Eric was shopping for himself and mingling with ladies.

While trying different fragrances in a bath and body works store, Eric met up with me and was begging me to come see this girl in the jewelry store. He said he didn't know if the guy she was with was her boyfriend, so he wanted me to come along just in case things got violent when he approached her in front of him. I argued with him explaining how I was different now and no matter how fine this girl was she wasn't worth the drama. He debated his point stating, "Yes she is, you've got to see her!" Although I told him I didn't want to see her because I had the perfect girlfriend, he went on and began describing this girls beauty from head to toe. As he described the thickness of her legs and this sexy anklet that she was wearing, I decided right then to get Ann an anklet because she liked them also!

As we approached the jewelry store I found out the girl Eric spoke of, was Ann! She was with a senior football star from her own high school, holding hands, kissing, and trying on jewelry. Eric had never met Ann before so he had no idea it was her and I couldn't tell him because I didn't want to face the ridicule and embarrassment on top of the pain associated with being betrayed by the one I loved and thought was perfect. I was crushed, so nauseated I felt like I was going to spew right there in the mall.

I was speechless and couldn't breathe however I pulled myself together and managed to get close enough to speak to Ann and her other lover. The minute we locked eyes she ran out of the mall crying and screaming. The guy she was with just looked at me with this look of confusion, I stared at him for a minute and then I shrugged my shoulders and walked off.

This was the turning point in my social life that would influence or dictate future relationships with the opposite sex for the duration of high school and some years afterwards. I became a cold hearted, uncompassionate, carefree, and cunning individual as it related to my interactions with women. The bad part is this seemed to be attractive to the women I dated, because no matter what the last one said about me, each new one came with the mindset of I wouldn't do that to them, or they could change me and every one received the same if not worse treatment then the last one.

Everything changed almost ten years later after meeting a Caucasian female that I fancied and she bore my first child. This little blessing would prove to be the miracle of a second chance at life by supplying heat to my ice-cold heart and giving me another chance at love. This beautiful baby girl was born November 20th, 2003 and even though her mother and I amicably grew apart the love that I've always received from my daughter has challenged me to be more mature in my personal life and to be more courteous, cautious and compassionate in the lives of other females.

After the split between her mother and me, I sunk into this deep depression and begin to lose all confidence in myself that I had acquired throughout this entire journey. I was broke, homeless, and a felon on child support, without a job. My only desire to stay alive and continue doing the right thing came from my daughter, so I used what I had at that time which was my music/ministry. After being taking under the wing of a charismatic youth pastor named Jamel Armstrong I put all I had into the ministries success.

Jamel became my best friend, pastor, ministry partner and first business manger. He was very instrumental in my survival at this stage in my life. While taking me with him to rap before he preached at various churches and events, I met a young lady named Cherrie Pointer who was over and involved in various ministries at her church.

Cherrie was putting together an event for Father's day and wanted to contract me to come do a spoken word piece. We met over my mother's house where I was living at the time, so she had the opportunity to meet my family out the gate. She took their comedic sarcasm well, instantly bonded with my younger sister (Sherrissa), and didn't completely loose her mind when a mouse ran across the living room floor. Although we both admit that in the beginning neither one of us viewed the other one as 'my type' yet we did have fun during the business meeting and because I was going through some family issues with my daughter's mother, we needed to clear the air so we went for a walk in Louisville Kentucky's downtown waterfront park. It was there that we begin to open up to one another personally about where we were in our lives. This was something that I usually didn't do because it made you vulnerable to the defense of the one you were planning to conquer if they knew your faults, weak points, frailties, etc. I guess because I didn't typically date church girls and felt I was way too rough around the edges for her, I didn't deem it to be necessary to revert to my usually tactics. It didn't take long for me to notice that it was something genuine about her heart and the compassionate concern that she expressed for me without even knowing who I was or all the dirt I'd done. There was a child-like innocence hidden in her beautiful smile that gave me a sense of security when discussing my journey with her, and an ever so comforting embrace in her arms as she held me, praying for me and speaking peace into my life as we prepared to call it a night and return to our respective homes. As, I went in and laid down I thought about how amazing of a person Cherrie was and although goody two-shoe church girls wasn't my type. I couldn't help but think about this short, chocolate, petite model shaped, bow-legged sistah who obviously knew a lot about fashion and lightweight had me off my game.

Cherrie and I stayed in touch as good friends after I fulfilled my contractual obligations to their church and it seemed as if during that whole season wherever I was invited or contracted to perform/minister I would run into her. Rather she was the main choreographer for a youth dance group or step team that was taking the stage, directing or leading a church choir, or just spear heading as one of the functions orchestrators or committee members. The more we saw each other the more we would contact each other and discuss/share information on events and opportunities. I put together this idea for a Christian mix tape using secular instrumentals and asked Cherrie to sing on one of the songs called "Won't Budge!"

This was the first song that we did together and it became really popular quite expeditiously. We begin ministering together on a regular basis when she wasn't busy with one of her many other ministries. Out of all her many gifts and talents, dancing is and always has been her favorite so when she got invited to do a dance workshop in Pensacola Florida she asked me to come along and minister with her. We went to a church called Deliverance Tabernacle and met some awesome people of God like C-the light and Tony Womack who a brother of ours in the faith named Monty Bussey set up. This ordained excursion would serve as proof that Cherrie and I was meant to be and ultimately would serve as the foundation of our ministry together.

As, we returned to Louisville and continued ministering together the past hurts and scars from previous relationships would sporadically surface making it almost impossible for me to believe that I found the one for me. I still was being haunted by the past of what I done and what was done to me, this caused doubt and fear thinking how every time I tried to play fair I ended up hurt. This hazardous train of thoughts influenced me to make some ignorant decisions and secretly justify them. I hadn't taken the time yet to do introspection and honestly research me, retracing my steps back through the painful places I didn't want to revisit in my life. However I had to do something because Cherrie left Louisville and went to Atlanta Georgia for a while giving me some time to see what I wanted to do about my future. It was during that time that I found and freed myself. I understood where I came from? Who I am? What I was and wanted to be? It didn't matter how many women I had at that time in my life none of them could fill the void inside me or assist in bringing forth the jewel that lied inside of me like Cherrie could. I needed and had to have her back! This is what allowed me to overcome the life-long fight I had been facing with myself. It took someone who was polar opposite from me, to look past my errors and still believe in the image of me that I couldn't see. The moral to this story is there is no such thing as the perfect girl or guy because we all are flawed individuals. I'm not discussing Cherries' flaws because that's beside the point. The point is even though there's no such thing as a perfect person there's someone who's perfect for you. However you have to realize it when it's in front of you, accept it, respect it, and do the mandatory personal inventory and labor if you really want it to work.

{ Side Note: When she returned to Louisville to visit, I proposed. Andre C. Barnes counseled and married us on March the 8th 2008. On that day I accepted her mess as she accepted mine and we vowed a covenant with God to mesh our messes and make something beautiful out of it that would glorify him. I'm not a perfect man but I love you Cherrie Vaughn and hope that you.

Don't change a thing boo-boo; you're perfect just the way you are! }

Chapter 9 "Ultimatum"

The Webster's College edition Dictionary describes an ultimatum as:

1. a final, uncompromising demand or set of terms issued by a party to a dispute,
2. a final proposal or statement of conditions.

Although I feel like this song is self-explanatory. For those who've never heard the song, or have but couldn't fully grasp and understand it, I will attempt to dissect and elaborate on this concept. We began this chapter defining what an ultimatum is, so for further clarification and to make sure we're all on one accord, I'll share a couple of examples to illustrate my point. Rather you realize it or not you've been handed ultimatums from the very beginning of your existence and you're faced with one that you must answer each day.

As an infant before your cognitive systems were developed enough to process verbal sound waves of information and respond accordingly, typically one of the first ultimatums you receive:

"You're going to take this bottle/pacifier or you're going to cry yourself to sleep!"

The statement is presented as a choice with no cause for contemplation because your options are limited and provided within:

"Complete all of your chores or you're not going anywhere!"

"You can either abide by my rules or get out of my house!"

You will face and answer ultimatums everyday of your life, and most commonly an ultimatum is set to persuade you to choose what's in your best interest or what's more comfortable for the one who sets the ultimatum. Your answer can be delayed however, when a real ultimatum is set there is no diverting or avoiding it, a decision must be made and more than likely followed with the appropriate action in a timely fashion.

Sometimes in life we give ourselves ultimatums. Before I actually knew what an ultimatum was I accepted one that could have been detrimental to my future. In the year 1999, to save some people who didn't give a damn about me I plead guilty to a felony charge of Complicity/Armed Robbery of a business and agreed to accept a plea bargain. The plea bargain itself was nothing other than a contractual ultimatum that I felt compelled to sign. It stated that I agreed to fully comply with the terms set forth by the Jefferson County judicial system or I would be reprimanded to serve out five years of penitentiary time. This was not a good deal however at the time of the proposal legally the cards were stacked against me. I had people snitching and lying at the same time saying it was me when they knew it wasn't, I had so called friends that were too scared to assist with my lawyer's impeccable defense and left me hanging at the last minute. Most importantly, I was too young to fully understand the severity of the situation or the repercussions of my actions. In my haste and ignorance I accepted this ultimatum, thinking by doing so it would make my problems go away, and although God graced me through this decision there would later arise more problems stemming from this one decision. For example, now that I was a felon and would have this blemish stained on every job applications criminal history section. Finding employment and making an honest living would be even more challenging than just being a young, black male without a degree, so if I didn't want to risk going to the penitentiary, either I would be under-employed or find a way to go back to school. This made me realize that sometimes we give and receive ultimatums, hoping that the answer will be the finale and provide closure to a problem, situation, or dispute. When in all actuality the answer to one ultimatum has the potential to lock you in a cycle of continuous ultimatums. Those five years that I spent tip-toeing through life, worried that one wrong move, could snatch me from my family by incarcerating my body and silencing my voice from the world. I'll never forget the embarrassment of being forced to submit to random drug tests and another man watching you urinate in a small container. Surprise probation officer visits at your job or place of residence where there better not be drugs, alcohol, or another felon present. I really hated job hunting with time restrictions, confessing to random strangers that I broke the law and even though I know you're not going to hire me, I need a signature from the manager or owner proving that I came in and applied today. You would think after facing all that and completing the term, maybe you could have somewhat I regular life again. Not happening! Because there is a stigma that follows you, even after completing your so-called debt to society. In whatever form you pay these dues to society, society will always label you by what you were and your chances for acknowledged rehabilitation, and publicly accepted redemption are slim to none. Therefore my advice is to never make uninformed decisions, especially when the decision can play a major role in determining the outcome of your future. It is your personal responsibility to acquire full disclosure and weigh every option and potential outcome before making any decisions. Remember this is your life, you only get one, and no one will respect yours if you don't!

That was a very challenging period in my life however the most difficult ultimatum that I've ever had to face came from someone who I really loved. This person and I had been intimate and in a committed relationship for at least five years. We lived together, shared everything, hardly ever fought and the few times that we did, it never lasted more than a couple of hours. I wasn't the best boyfriend because I was still maturing and dealing with a lot of the personal issues of self I already discussed. But I was willing to sacrifice myself to make the relationship work and did my best to keep my girl happy. After investing so much time and energy into each other, we discussed starting a family and taking our relationship to the next level. It was at this point when she allowed me to know that she had grown very uncomfortable with my choice of career in entertainment. She acknowledged it as my true passion, one of the few things that I had ever been persistent in attempting to accomplish, and confessed although she'd felt like this for some time she couldn't say anything because she knew how much my music meant to me. However now that we were discussing marriage and starting a family of our own she felt compelled to me tell that she never viewed herself as the wife/mother of a traveling entertainer who, may or may not be home this week. She stated, "I love you for who you are and always will, but if we're going to be together you have to give up your pipe dreams and work a regular full-time shift like everyone else!" Although I was devastated and confused because I was in love, I totally understood where she was coming from and respected the fact that she was being flat-foot honest with me. I kind of wished she would've told me sooner before I allowed myself to fall completely head over heels. But at this point none of that mattered because, I knew that with this ultimatum either way it went I was going to lose a love. This was hands down the hardest decision that I've ever had to make and I still deal with the effects of my answer every day of my life. No matter how much I loved her, music was a part of my destiny, and to even attempt to shut it off would be like taking breathe from my lungs and purpose from my soul. Without a second guess or exhaustive contemplation I told her I loved her and always will but our path together had ran its course and must end. I collected what I needed for my journey into the unknown, turned around and walked out never to return. There's not much more to say about that situation, other than at the end of the day, I want it to be known that I'm very big on family! Any decisions that I've ever made that directly or indirectly involved my family or extensions thereof were very perplexing, stressful, and overall taxing. Because I love my family tree! Every root, branch, limb, stem and leaf without question, favoritism, or prejudice…End of story!

Ironically, it wouldn't be long before a similar ultimatum pertaining to my career would be presented to me by another female. This one ,however, was different because it came across as positive, heart-felt, and it convicted me in my spirit afterwards. I'm paraphrasing but it went something like this:

"Sam I love you, trust you, and believe in you. Not just as an artist but as an individual. You have the potential to make an impact that would leave a mark on this world to be remembered forever. Yet you choose to do nothing, be nothing, and have nothing so that no one knows you and those who do forget you. I'm willing to stand with you rather you decide to be a gospel rapper, gangster rapper, or a bus driver. But I love you too much to stand here and watch you self-destruct in my presence! I'm leaving for a while so that you can have some time and space to think about what you really want out of life. Get it together or I'm gone forever!"

This speech was delivered by my then girlfriend Cherrie Pointer before taking that trip to Atlanta I told you about. Six months later, I proposed and she became my wife. Even today, I still consider this speech the most eloquent and inspirational ultimatum I've ever received. This ultimatum would reverberate in my spirit each day I spent without her and made me question how I was living and what I really wanted from life? This was the first time in my life that I had been intimately involved with a woman who loved and believed in me so much that I felt compelled to completely elevate my status. I truly desire to be and consistently labor towards becoming an all around better man.

This is the answer to the question people always ask, "Why did you get married? Or how did you know that she was the one?" The same answer applies to both questions, because she makes me strive to be a better person within myself at anything and everything that I do, while accepting me for who I am.

Now with that being said, within two years of being married my unaddressed issues with my self-esteem, ego, and insecurities led me down a path where I once again devalued myself. The result was I defaced what I had. Eventually, my secrets led to dishonesty, my dishonesty led to infidelities, and my infidelities led to another ultimatum of losing my family. If you've ever heard the actual song "Ultimatum" then you know that the first verse captured the raw but true sentiment of what I was experiencing. I knew that Cherrie was supposed to be my wife and never doubted the love that we shared. However because I hadn't dealt with my personal issues, I was involuntarily allowing my own flaws to destroy what we were building, and I had no defense for these random attacks of self because I didn't know when or why they'd strike. I had to retrace my steps back to the beginning of my pain. I didn't want to face it again or admit to it, in order to realize that I had a serious problem with being faithful in a committed relationship. This had been plaguing me since junior high school. Being able to locate the origin of the issue helped me to understand why I behave a certain way and what triggers these feelings and outbursts. This didn't stop or put an end my nature however I was able to monitor, explain and maintain better control over these issues than previously.

I'll probably never be perfect in this aspect yet I will strive to achieve it and I promise you with that mindset alone, instead of blaming my exes and justifying my actions of pain, my family and I are a lot better off.

{Side Note: It's a rough and continuous path you must walk in this process of becoming what you're called to be and being able to adapt is very important because this path is full of shifts and transitions that are mandatory in order to live out your fullest potential. As, I think about the earlier stages of the process and what came with constructing the "Face 2 Face" project, I believe this song "Ultimatum" was the foundation for the entire project. I say this because the concept and idea for this song as well as the entire project came to me after Cherie's ultimatum was made during a period of solitude. }

After being invited to minister musically and orchestrate a creative arts workshop at Deliverance Tabernacle in Pensacola, Florida, Cherrie and I grew closer in our ministry and our personal lives. So, we began dating. The ministry was received well by the congregation of Deliverance Tabernacle and we were asked to return the following year. Weighing our options, we agreed that they were great people and we had an awesome time so we accepted the invitation. We returned to Pensacola that following year and by this time Cherrie and I was in a serious committed relationship.

Our ministries and personal lives had merged as we became very comfortable ministering together, which at that point we had been doing consistently for about two years. Just as it had before, the ministry went forth well at Deliverance Tabernacle, so well that we were invited by the church's audio technician to return to Pensacola for a third time to his recording studio. He had a very professional studio that was located on church grounds and he promised to engineer our entire album for free if we returned with the instrumentals. This engineer was no stranger to major productions his name was Curry Smith or a.k.a "C-the light" who had spent years in New York working for various labels in the early 90's, such as with Viacom. While in his hometown of the Big Apple following his dreams, he received and answered his call into the ministry. This left him no other option but to walk away from the fame and fortune of the secular music industry, dedicate his life to Jesus Christ, and accept his divine assignment to serve God's people in Pensacola Florida. After doing our diligence, researching and verifying this information Cherrie and I counted this opportunity as a blessing of the Lord to be explained as the favor of God operating on our lives and in our ministry.

    We considered it an honor as we returned to Louisville and visited three of my cousins, who all in their own right were musical geniuses with totally different styles, as it related to instrumental song composition and music/beat production. Mike, Ken, and Gary Silver are three of four brothers who are siblings of my deceased big cousin Monte that I discussed in chapter one. (The fourth one is Wesley who also raps but is the only one who doesn't make beats.) Between these three musically inclined minds of brethren, Cherrie and I received fourteen instrumentals free of charge that later we would write to, record on, and produce with C- the light in Pensacola. After the completion of this project, we brainstormed over the tracks, the ministry, and our purpose and titled this album "Save Our Streets (S.O.S)." Mind you this is before our marital engagement or commencement so it was probably around summer of 2005 when this album was completed in production. Now because C-the light was very busy as were we, usually all the edit approvals and correspondence dealing with the "S.O.S." project was handled via internet or United Stated mail. This would prove to be a very lengthy process, that before we actually got to the end, it would ultimately be two years and two trips to Florida later. By this time we were married, parents to our first son, travelling and ministering with a separate project produced in Louisville Kentucky called "The

Crippled Soundtrack." This was a mix-tape style collection of musical works, that derived from the first book written by our dear friend and pastor who would later officiate our wedding Andre C. Barnes. This project opened many doors for us and our fresh but flourishing, unique style of ministry. At the same time we finally received the finalized "S.O.S" project from Pensacola and was preparing ourselves to be open and ready for whatever God was about to do through us by our union, spirits, hearts, and our ministry.

It was at this crucial point in our ministry that my issues not only showed up but exposed themselves as a serious problem. These issues of self had become a problem that I could no longer conceal, because it had taken over my better judgment and honestly I was just incapable of handling it at this point. My secret lifestyle became less private as I received phone calls, texts, and emails that were intercepted by my wife. After conversations were held and information was shared a lot of my secrets turned out to be dishonest cover-ups and my deceitful maneuvers to feed my fleshes sinful desires created a happily married man of God who struggled with infidelities and was on the verge of losing everything I'd worked so hard to build. I can't imagine all the mental and emotional stress my wife was under but I understand her reason for wanting to separate from me and any mutual connections thereof. This included but was not limited to, our home, ministry, relationship and music, so even though this package had arrived from Pensacola that we'd been waiting two years to receive it was all worthless! Initially I tried self-justifying my actions and managed to play it cool for about a week or two without my family. After the loneliness set in, it brought guilt realizing that the conditions of my circumstances was by fault of my own. It was then that I began slipping into this deep manic depressive state. I figured the best person for me to be with at that point in my life, was the one who could probably relate the best with what I was going through emotionally. Out of fear from the suicidal thoughts I was experiencing, I decided to do something I'd never done which was move in with my father, Sam. This was a great learning and humbling experience for me because I typically wrote him off, as most of the family did as crazy or weak for shooting himself. However now that I was in a state of vulnerability and battling with similar demonic spirits, I just felt compelled to boldly ask.

"Daddy, I always told myself that one day I was going to ask you this question and today is the day. Did you really want to die? What made you shoot yourself?" My father turned and looked at me with confidence before replying, "I didn't know who I was, I knew who I had to be as far as my wife, family, military, and etc was concerned however I didn't know me!"

"It felt as if I was running 1000 miles an hour non-stop in every direction but wasn't covering any ground. I was going absolutely nowhere extremely fast and no matter what or how much I did it never seemed to be enough to satisfy me or the people I was trying so hard to please. I'm sorry you have to hear this but honestly, at that point in my life yes I wanted to die if it meant that it all would stop. I just wanted it all to stop!"

I was completely speechless because twenty something years later I was standing were my father stood, maybe for a different reason however contemplating the same fate and it was the one whom I least expected to help me through this ultimatum.

God spoke to me that night and gave me the ultimatum of trusting him and living a life of abundance or denying him and choosing Satan which meant certain death. On my knees in the floor of my father's guest room, with a snotty nose from crying what seemed to be endless tears, I chose to live and received these instructions:

"Close yourself off from everybody and purge yourself in music. This music will not be genre specific and will contain the duality of manhood along with the struggle between spirit and flesh in transition to position my people for real salvation. This will be the first of four albums that you will release under this concept and it won't be easy attempting to serve me and bridge the gaps between my people. However I'll be with you every step of the way as long as you go forth walking in spirit and in truth."

As I awoke that night from a vision of death, darkness and catacombs, I walked into the bathroom shaking with fear. As I washed my face, while looking in the mirror I saw two different reflections. One I say was in a fleshy form (Klypto), because it was glimpse of my image in my former life in the streets. The other I say was in a spiritual form (SaMajesty), because it was an image of myself that although I could see, I couldn't be because it seemed to be pure and righteous. Thus the concept for the first CD was birthed "Face 2 Face". This is an honest look and testimony of who I am without condemnation or approval from anyone. There are days where I feel like "I'm on fire in the spirit of the Holy ghost / ..." and there are other days where I feel like "I'm from the city / the city, city/... and we go hard!" Regardless of; what I sing, how I dress or talk, what beliefs, customs, or teachings I'm partial to, at the end of the day, there's only one who can judge. The real question is do you know him enough to bet your eternity on who and what he's approved. I understand my purpose and reason for existence. I'm dedicated and committed to walking it out fully and unapologetically. The song "Ultimatum" itself was a collaborative effort between me and my younger cousin, Mike Silver.

We had a powerful discussion about ultimatums and the choices we must make in life and how some can create peace or war. I began writing the verses after he came up with that powerful chorus section that would later be revamped by the lead of a rock band, and please forgive me for not remembering the name of the band.

As it relates to the church, I've been asked so many questions and received much backlash for being so personal and honest on this song. I've had people come up to me and say, "It's not healthy for a Christian to share those types of struggles with the unsaved. Some things should only be between you and God!"

I've also had people come up to me and say, "That song was a blessing to my marriage because I thought no one understood what I was going through and by hearing your song about it, I was able to change and keep my family."

At the end of the day one must realize that you'll never be able to please everybody. Anytime that you're doing a new thing there are always going to be some hell raisers, who'll be set on making some smoke in the city about what you're doing. However when the dust settles and the smoke clears my ultimate goal is to reach ultima-Thule, which is described as a Latin word meaning 'the highest degree attainable, or the farthest point; the limit to any journey.' I plan to accomplish this by answering the most important and ultimately the only ultimatum that really matters however I'm going to put it in the form of a question. Regardless of your personal habits, feelings, battles etc, when called upon will you or will you not serve the most high? I answered yes to the most high and received back all I had lost due to my own ignorance with interest. However it did take a few ultimatums and making the right decisions in response to them in order for things to line up with the universe.

In essence ultimatums can be a great tool of inspiration or motivation for one to challenge themselves toward self elevation and the achievement of greatness. If I may offer advice it would be forget about what people have to say about you and your character, follow God and watch the mysteries of the universe be unveiled before your very eyes. Most importantly along with peace, liberation, and salvation, the joys of your heart shall be given unto you.

I pray you receive this, in Jesus Name…Amen

Chapter 10 "Goin All Out"

No longer will I allow myself or anyone else to hold me back from greatness. I refuse to sit quietly on my gifts, dumb down my spirit or character, and continue to ignore the wide ranged versatility of my personality. From this moment forward, I declare with the utter most confidence, that whatever I'm doing I will push it to the limits, in an attempt to perform each task to the best of my ability and at full capacity in hopes of breaking all chains and leaving no holds barred. May this declaration unto God also serve as a glorious celebration of self revelation and redemption! I intend to go all out and the picture that I desire to illustrate would be one set in the evening around a beautifully decorated, extravagant nightclub, where everyone is made to feel like a superstar. There would be front door chauffer and valet services. Paparazzi cameras would flicker and flash from the moment you stepped out of your vehicle. While live media footage would be rolling from impromptu interviews, as you stroll down a red carpet in between velvet ropes. Comforted by the fact, that you'll be presidentially protected by personal bodyguards, who've been trained to perform with a secret service styled security detail. You will have the opportunity to mingle amongst A-list clientele, celebrities, and top level officials and officers, who'd be dressed in their best wardrobes of expensive delicate fabrics, and high-stepping through the doors of the main entrance. This entrance would lead into an upscale ballroom with a live band and deejay working together on the playlist which would include various genres and styles of music. Wine and some alcoholic beverages would be served in moderation but closely supervised by the house for Christian accountability. This would be an evening where adults would be free to socialize, network and fellowship in a classy party-like atmosphere in an environment that would be comfortable enough for all citizens and secure enough for all Christians to attend.

It's a widely known and a commonly accepted fact that I'm a dreamer so I may just be wishful thinking. However it's shameful for followers of Christ to live like or believe their not entitled to party or enjoy themselves. What's worse is the fact of when they do party or cut loose, they feel the need to hide from their brethren because they don't want to be ridiculed, shamed, or embarrassed. Typically what happens is they end up going where the heathens go, and act how the heathens act attempting to just have some fun and blend in. This rose the question in my spirit of, Is it humanly possible to party or celebrate in the nightlife without compromising your faith or beliefs? Some would think so because not only are celebrations biblical but Jesus himself attended a few. I think the major issue is having a personal relationship with God that's strong enough, to keep you conscious and mindful to know thyself, your boundaries and limitations. Therefore maintaining the balance of self, and God's will, with the power to govern yourself accordingly. This phrase may mean different things to different people depending on where you are in your personal life. For instance one person may need the opportunity to have an alcoholic beverage to settle anxieties and feel liberated, while another may have to be extremely cautious because one drink is an open invitation for them to get stumbling drunk. There may be one who could use the confidence booster or companionship of a nice dance from the opposite sex, and then there's always the one who's going to turn every dance or opportunity to engage the opposite sex into a strip tease or freak fest. I guess the question that I'm posing is, Can you party with class and tact? Or does the idea of having fun equate with sin or constitute you must wild out? I would obviously say of course not but that's only in the lane of being able to speak for myself. At the end of the day we all are in pursuit of something however, we go about retrieving it in different ways, due to the different points of transition we are in, in our own personal lives. Therefore we must be cautious that in our own liberation we're not condemning anyone else. Yet we can't allow ourselves to be condemned in the process of our own liberation neither. It's a very slippery slope that we must climb but I'm comforted by a sermon delivered by Pastor Andre C. Barnes entitled in the absence of perfection, be honest! Understand that your walk is your walk, and wherever you're at in that walk is a part of your own personal process of salvation. Everything that is deemed as sin to you and may constitute missing the mark, may not yield or equal the same results for someone else. The bottom line once again, is to know thyself and be honest with yourself and others about where you are in your walk. Be there to minister or pray with others but don't try to make them you. Allow them to find themselves in God and challenge them to endure their own personal process.

During the initial creative process of this song, I met with the phenomenal beat maker and musical producer Ricky 'Boom' Whittington who was responsible for creating more than 60% of the instrumentals for the entire "Face 2 Face" project. When I first sat down and began to vibe with the music, before I attempted to write any lyrics, I felt the music had the swag of relationships and sexiness, so it was originally decided to be the song "Ms. Perfect." However after reciting and discussing the lyrics with Boom, we mutually agreed to swap the lyrics to "Perfect" with another track and create something different for this instrumental.

The main idea was to capture the classical Jazz feeling of the music and mesh it with a confident, mature swag to create a song with a more upscale grown and sexy feel of Hip-Hop. We knew this meant it probably wouldn't meet the requirements of a typical Christian Rap song, yet giving my status, beliefs, and personal convictions it couldn't be what's considered an average Rap song neither. We understood from the very beginning this song would be totally out of the box and potentially controversial. For the most part, he came up with an idea and after I grasped the concept, we collaborated with our minds, talents, and resources to make this vision a reality.

First, he requested the assistance of fellow musicians that he played with in the Totally Dedicated Band. These guys were professional, gifted musicians, who didn't hesitate to come to the studio the same day and assist Boom with this personal project. All it took was the passion for music and the love for each other that those guys shared and the true sentiment of the song began to unfold. That's how it morphed into the composition that you know, listen to, and love today.

Writing the lyrics became easier by the minute because I kept the mentality of when I was hustling in the streets and stunted with the real high-rollers as if I was balling. In those days we would host these narcissist parties where everything was based around me and my team. We would dress, talk, and act as if we were modern day mobsters with the heart of the streets, the game on lock, and the city eating out of the palm of our hands. This attitude and display of expression is still very common amongst party planners and promotional teams today. As you know, image is everything and this concept was sort of the imagery we desired to convey however, this time it would be submerged in the idea of positivity and prestige founded on the basis legitimacy. We wanted to create a shifting paradigm because often when people think of a party now days it's engulfed in sin. Rather it's the hustler's blood money that funds the festivities or the drug and sexual innuendos that's being pitched to its participants. Being that we were from the streets, we understood the streets, and wanted to keep the essence of the streets included. Our reasoning came from the knowledge of realizing they're known for throwing the best parties and with our individual ministries in motion, these were the people we desired to impact. Our problem was, not wanting to be false representatives or fake as it relates to either side. ***Being from the streets we understand the terminology, lifestyle, ways, and culture. However we're no longer a part of it and even though we are believers of Christ that understand the terminology, lifestyle, ways, and culture of the modern day church, that's not us either! I can only speak for myself but somewhere in the middle of street life and church life is where I am. I'm not a thug nor am I church boy!*** Therefore, we wanted to put a spin on the concept of a players' ball that could be organized by legitimate business men, hosting a mature upscale celebration for positive and hard-working people.

This is a rare and complicated concept, the ability to showcase the most popular yet the most derogatory musical genre (Hip-Hop) in a positive but not churchy way, would prove itself to be one of the biggest challenges we faced in putting this album together. We felt this challenge was mandatory because of the need to show the church hip hop's relevance in ministry and witness to the streets, that spirituality is a necessary commodity for this modern culture. Our hope is to bridge the gaps between the church and the streets, while simultaneously reprogramming minds by reformatting music and spotlighting a typically untapped market. Our goal is to prove that when created, promoted, and distributed correctly. Clean music would show itself to be lucrative for us, as well as profitable to the music industry as a whole. In order to understand my ministry, you must understand that I am a visionary with the heart to impact all people and I'm in seek of a revolution that will ultimately change the game all together. In order to accomplish this goal we must be willing to face the music that's out there and understand that all of it is not going to be Jesus music however, for our children's sake it would be wise and in the best interest of us all, to clean it up a little. No matter how many churches or Christian events I support, perform in or attend this has always been my lane as an artist, to create music that's healthy, classic, and revolutionary.

I've been cautioned by my mentors on many occasions about creating and maintaining some sort of balance in my business and personal life. I believe that as an artist, it is imperative that musically I provide a balance. Therefore, there are songs on my album that will make you party, as well as songs that will make you worship and everything in between. With that being said I must confess that "Goin All Out" is my least favorite song on the album, and if I had to be honest the reason would probably be because it's the furthest from my comfort zone.

This one particular song really pushed the envelope and challenged me professionally as an artist/writer. It was the very last song to be completed on the album and almost got removed afterwards if it hadn't been for the expertise of Boom and the Totally Dedicated band. This is the one song on the album that always surprises me when someone says that it's there favorite. Before cutting the song from the album all together, there was a big discussion and we agreed that on every album that we've bought or just listened to, there is always a song that blows you away and a song that makes you wonder how it made the final cut, and typically the song that you wonder how it made the final cut is the song that blows someone else away and vice versa. I guess the theory behind this revelation is that everything isn't for everybody, however just because it's not for you doesn't mean it's not for anybody! That is the mysterious beauty of music, it can become whatever the artist or interpreter makes it and I was told by a fellow artist years ago that I don't make music because I am music.

The great author/composer Ray Bradbury said, "Writing lets the world burn through you!" Judging by some of the music that's being broadcasted throughout the world right now I would hope not, however knowing that because I'm a heartfelt mc everything I feel, see, and experience goes into my music so I'm forced to agree with Mr. Bradbury. As an artist who creates music and manages to stay true to himself, there's something special about connecting to another person who's from a totally different walk of life and creating a bond through the music.

This reminds me of one evening while shopping at a local Louisville grocery store, while in the fresh produce aisle getting some vegetables for dinner, one of the store employees stepped in front of my shopping cart and greeted me ecstatically. This guy was a short, chubby, middle-aged African-American male with a balding head and raspy voice. He began by asking a question that he answered himself, "Are you? Yeah, SaMajesty I knew that was you!" His name was Rayshawn and he spent twenty minutes talking to me about how much the ministry of my wife and I had blessed him every time he'd witnessed us in action. How beautiful we are as a couple and how inspirational it was to see us unified in love and operating in our gifts. This conversation led to him asking for some relationship advice and transitioned to a musical consultation, as he began singing in the middle of the grocery aisle asking me what I thought of singing and songwriting skills. The conversation ended with the store manager coming over and attempting to reprimand Rayshawn but I spoke so highly of his patience, manners, and desire to please the customers he ultimately was promoted. We exchanged numbers and still keep in touch from time to time.

But immediately after getting my vegetables, before making it to the checkout counter I was approached by another middle-aged man named Bill who was a muscular, blonde-haired Caucasian. He noticed my stage name and company logo on my sweatshirt and said, "I just wanted to shake your hand and congratulate you on an awesome album."

I replied in disbelief posing the question, "You've heard my album?"

Bill said, "Yes, and before hearing your Rap album I never liked that type of music."

That wasn't the first time I heard one of my elders make a similar statement yet, I was intrigued enough to inquire what sparked Bills' interest in my music so I asked.

He said, "Initially I seen you and your wife singing a beautiful song on television for the WHAS Crusade for Children and because I have a special needs child who reaps all kinds of benefits from that organization it really touched me. Two days later I was still singing it and decided to search for the song online. When I found the song it was on an album called Face 2 Face and I figured why not listen to the whole album since I liked the Crusade song so much! I listened to it, loved it, purchased it, and still play it almost every day. Probably my favorite song on the entire album now is Goin All Out. It changed my relationship with my kids because I hated Rap, and they loved it, but now they look at me as the cool parent because we all enjoy your Rap album and we dance around the house together. Not only can I dance to it, but I can understand and relate to what you're saying because you're really saying something, and I just wanted to thank you for that. Keep up the good work SaMajesty and when you get to the top please don't forget the old white guy... Bill!"

This wasn't the first or the last time that I experienced an encounter like this, however every time I think of the song "Goin All Out" I can't help but picture Bill and his family dancing around their house. This makes me think of my own family and while each and every member is going all out in their own unique yet significant ways, I'm forced to surround my final thoughts on this concept around my step-father Cedric Threat who I call Pap.

I remember when I first started rapping and trying to make a name for myself, Pap made the same comment about this career choice as he did everything else I attempted and believed would prosper me.

"Get bigger than the hood!" This was the popular phrase shared between us that inspired me to believe in myself and push beyond the atmosphere because the sky isn't the limit! It didn't matter how large or small the accomplishment was, anytime I would make a move that meant some type of elevation in my career, I would call or visit Pap and share with him the entire story. All though every one of my stories may have had undeniable similarities, each one was unique in its own way. Yet and still every conversation that Pap and I shared for some reason always ended the same. With all the confidence in the world he would stare into me with proud parental eyes, nodding his head in approval, and calmly reply, "Yes, Sir. Get bigger than the hood!"

Those of you who can't relate to how it feels to be a young black male, who's raised in a impoverished household, as a victim of circumstances or his surroundings, losing all hope while being targeted by law enforcement, hunted by your own kind, and trapped between cold-hearted women, homosexuals, and the walls of your own mind. To be stereotyped on a regular basis as someone so negative people look down on you or fear the thought of you approaching them. I speak of brothers groomed in ghetto protocol, which typically means they have roots that stem from the criminal underworld. That were taught by survivors, who refused to let the oppression of living beneath their means on the low end of the financial scales, and accept the responsibility of bearing the load for a money hungry capitalistic society. A society who, refuses to acknowledge the labor and legacy of their ancestors that literally gave their life for the sake of building this country. Because of these reasons and others, they chose the option of attempting to create a life in an unforgiving sub-culture, as a means of success and survival for their families. You would think that these citizens would be offered some type of assistance or rehabilitation because America as a whole has failed them.

Instead these young men are physically, mentally, socially, and economically abused and because they learn to adapt and survive in the world they're taught. They become the enemy as they're labeled, targeted, and issued a decree of death from birth. "Get bigger than the hood!" This is not a statement that pertains to your geographical location but an over comers philosophy directly dealing with one's own conscious state of mind. That's why you see so many celebrities who've risen from the bottom and infiltrated the ranks of the upper class but never renewed or freed their mind from the stigma of ghetto mentality and ultimately this becomes their downfall.

Getting bigger than the hood isn't how much money you make, what you have, who you know, or what you've accomplished. To Pap over coming this mentality was the first step to rising above living a lifestyle of defeat and accepting the complacency of mediocrity which is common amongst most bottom dwellers. Pap always told me that the only way out of the hood for good, was to defeat the same mentality that you must use to survive in the hood. In my maturity and increased level of understanding I know that a lot of readers are lost right now because they know nothing about the hood, let along surviving it! Therefore, I will attempt to share with you all some of the most basic yet pertinent rules of hood survival…

- Stay Focused- everyone has a gimmick, idea, scheme or something they want to solicit your assistance in doing. You must know who you are, what you believe, and what is your

ultimate goal? Let nothing or no one deter or distract you from reaching your goal.
- Observe- Pay attention to details. This includes actions, conversations, places etc. Be studious because you never know what information is important or detrimental, until you need it and don't have it.
- Humble Confidence- Humility allows you to gain others trust and respect which often raises your likeability. However always be assured in yourself, you don't need anyone else's validation. This makes you a leader and limits the times you'll be lead a stray.
- Respect- Everybody, every situation and yourself. This rule is one of the most important ones, so make sure you understand what this statement means. Violation in the wrong situation could be detrimental or force immediate death!
- Keep it Real- Or in layman terms, just be honest and be you wherever you are unless rule #4 must be applied. Understand that it is impossible for everyone to like you, so don't lose sleep or run around trying to please everybody, it only makes matters worse.
- Relate and don't judge- Do not separate or detach yourself from the people. Find a common bond, past or present. Use terms like us and we, instead of you or them. Never say, what you wouldn't do or speak badly of someone else's doing. Choose your words wisely.
- Compassionate communication- Understand that others may not agree with you or understand your feelings. Being able to accept where they are yet, effectively convey your message, how you feel and leave it alone. Be careful not to press or force any issues that aren't mandatory. This could result in serious consequences, if you don't know how to gauge that persons' level of tolerance.

- Negative Optimism- What can go wrong will go wrong! Even though your situation is bad, potentially it could get worse. You must always believe that it can and will get better. There is always a better way, you just have to keep a cool head and find it.
- Will to fight- They say violence isn't an option but I say, violence isn't the first option. There will be times when you must go to war and be willing to die for your cause or beliefs. "A man who has nothing to fight for has no reason to live." – MLK. He continues saying, "a man who stands for nothing will fall for anything."
"Some corners you will be backed into and forced to come out fighting, if you plan on coming out!
- Loyal self-preservation- Always have your peoples back! If we came together then we leave together. At the end of the day, no matter what you've done or doing, your top priority is to make it home safely! You never know when you're going to need somebody, and living in the hood eventually you will. Just make sure the loyalty factor is mutually shared with all you give it too!

These were ten rules of surviving the hood that Pap instilled in me as a father hoping to see his son make it through the dangerously chaotic lifestyles of hood life and it is these same ten rules one must reference to rise above the mentality that plaques the urban community. I'm grateful for Pap being there to share the wisdom of his knowledge and experiences with me, while at the same time accepting nothing short of success from me without excuses. After years of blood, sweat, tears, challenges, prayers, and blessings from the Lord.

Finally, I can see the light at the end of the tunnel in the form of progression. I haven't arrived yet and as my elders always said, 'the struggle continues' but now I can truly relate to 2pac's poem of "The Rose that Grew from Concrete." I've been tempted, tested, and tried in the fire yet I rose from the flames and took flight like the Greek mystical bird, the Phoenix. There's no telling what the future holds for me or for you. I just ask that we collectively declare that we're "Goin' All Out" and in unification "Get bigger than the hood!"

Chapter 11 "Remember My Name"

As a young man, there were many times that I didn't get my way, or things didn't happen quite like I felt they should've, and whenever this turn of events took place I would lash out. Running off, crying, pouting, etc. If I wasn't giving you the silent treatment then, I was probably ranting and raving about how I deemed the matter to be unfair. I was considered to have a real bad attitude and was often spoke of as an 'army brat' or the spoiled child. Although I couldn't accept it back then, in retrospect I know it was the truth, and it didn't take much to set me off either because I was the worst sore loser. I was a fierce competitor that turned everything into a competition, and I had to win even if it was just in my mind. For most people it isn't or wasn't that serious but, for me it was extremely serious. For example, if I didn't come out victorious when challenged at a video game I would repeatedly throw the game controller against the floor, strike myself, or attempt to fight the winner. This would happen almost instantly, without any gloating or provocation from the one who defeat me.

There were a few times when my mother threatened to have me evaluated by a psychiatrist because of my reactions to loosing or not being the best at something. I thank God that she never actually took me because, there are many of our kids who are misdiagnosed with false, or fake mental illnesses such as ADHD, just because the major pharmaceutical companies offer kickbacks to the medical providers and parents who're willing to dope up the children. The ways that I was acting out, regardless of everything I was going through back then, I'm sure any doctor would've had me medicated to the point where I was incapacitated, drooling down my chin and talking to the walls.

The most embarrassing story that my family still teases me about today took place at one of my elementary school's field days. If you don't know what a field day is, it's where the entire school is split into teams by their own classrooms and then they compete against teams from other classes in their grade level. The competition usually includes various outdoor challenges, containing sports and obstacle courses. Upon completion of field day, awards are given to the top three overall performing teams, and everyone else receives a ribbon or certificate of participation. For most of the children who were involved, a day away from the classroom where they were able to have fun outdoors was rewarding enough, but for the youth who were very competitive like myself and hated to lose, it meant so much more. On this field day, I was placed on a team with a fellow female classmate who was physically handicapped. She wore braces on both of her legs that enabled her to walk. After a day of competing, giving my best and almost flawlessly winning each challenge set before me. Due to our entire team performance, we ended up needing to win the final challenge in order to receive an overall first place ranking. The final challenge was a team relay race and I had a teammate who's, personal challenge limited her physical capabilities and caused the team as a whole to be ineffective competitively. Needless to say our team didn't win field day that year and because I was such a sore loser that was accustomed to winning I displayed the worst sportsmanship like conduct in the history of competition. I refused to accept my ribbon of participation while throwing a toddlers tantrum ranting and raving about how I was the best competitor on the field. As if that wasn't ridiculous enough I went further in disrespect by dishonoring myself, family, and team insulting the efforts of my handicap teammate who only desired to participate and feel like a normal child. To this very day, I'm still ridiculed by my family for the selfish ignorance that I displayed that afternoon, and in retrospect their jokes pale in comparison to the shame felt when thinking of how I must've made that young lady feel. While in the moment, I was too immature to understand this concept so all I could think of, was myself. How much I wanted to win, and therefore, how unfair this was for me.

Throughout my adolescence anytime I didn't get my way or things didn't go the way that I felt they should've for me the first three words to be projected from my lips were, "That's not fair!" As long as I was happy or was receiving what I desired then life was beautiful, but anytime I wasn't there was hell to pay, because I was irate, belligerent, and sometimes violent with revenge feeling mistreated screaming something 'wasn't fair!'

My mother broke me from that train of thought by always replying with this philosophy. "Fair, what's fair? Get fair out of your mind because life isn't fair and it never will be! Nobody cares about a poor, angry, little black boy screaming what's fair. The closest you'll ever get to life being fair for you is through the will and ability to change some things and the only way to do that is to put yourself in a position where people will listen to you. So my suggestion to you is instead of always crying and complaining about what is and isn't fair, channel that energy into putting yourself on a platform where people will listen to what you have to say and actually have something to say that'll change things!"

I didn't know this at the time however that has become an adopted philosophy and major goal in my life. I recognize the injustice, hardships, and inequalities mutually shared amongst us all and I admit that judicial work, politics, and policies aren't my strong suit. Yet, I've come to understand the idolizing leadership of celebrities and the undeniable true spiritual power of the amplified human voice. This is why I've dedicated the rest of my life to utilizing these practical qualities along with whatever else I've been endowed with, to put myself in a position where people will listen to me. Each day I become closer to achieving this goal with the understanding of a bigger responsibility to make sure that I'm saying something worth listening to. I chose music because it holds the unprecedented potential to impact everyone in some shape, form, or fashion. This makes music the perfect vessel to use when attempting to deliver an audible message to large numbers of people simultaneously. My decision to utilize the genre of Hip-Hop is due to the fact that it's my personal favorite and it's still the largest and fastest growing form of artistic expression in the world today.

Ironically over thirty years ago when it was originated on the East Coast it wasn't expected to last. It was written off as an uninteresting African-American ghetto fad that was meaningless and projected to die well before the turn of the century. Obviously the critics and skeptics were wrong, the evidential fact that not only is it still alive but it is also expanding, and becoming more lucrative each year. This is probably because Hip-Hop has found a way to mesh with all other genres of music, crossing all age, race, and geographical barriers. In addition to being adopted by most businesses and organizations as a marketing/advertisement tool. This raises the question in my head, if everyone else can push their message through the medium of Hip-Hop why can't I? Hip-Hop is not dead! It lives and breathes just like any other organism on Earth. Influencing every aspect of human life the way we socialize, dress, behave and etc. In my personal opinion this art form has took over the world! Most importantly, it will determine what our future will be because its hands hold the hearts and minds of our children and occupies the majority of this current generation. Have you noticed that America's youth typically view music videos as the most important program on television? Many of them know more Rap lyrics than basic scholastic education and more celebrity news than local news and current events combined. This makes it impossible to fathom why certain political, educational, and spiritual institutions refuse to acknowledge and utilize this power tool of communication.

How can you plan to be successful and effective having longevity dealing with the youth without incorporating this tool at all. My idea is not just use it but master it and gain certification, validation, and approval from the future leaders of the free world with it. I practice vigorously without tire knowing that the balance of someone's salvation may weigh on my ability to properly convey the lyrical word of God in such a manner that it convicts and ministers to their heart. This could ultimately be the difference between them choosing God right now or waiting until later when later is too late.

For the record this is not a game to me, I don't consider myself a Christian artist but an artist who is a Christian and I pray that I don't have to spend so much time rapping or speaking it because it's visually apparent. That's why I don't feel like every composition or spoken word has to be filled with Bible scriptures or include Jesus' name. I understand that sometimes you have to meet people right where they are and subtle messages behind compassion and correlation typically will get the job done. This type of ministry where I'm from is called bait music. Something attractive dangled in front of the catch that as soon as they grab it they're hooked and you just reel them in. As, they begin to mature in their faith they'll request or demand more substance in their spiritual diets. I know this concept may seem absurd and I probably would agree with you if this was something that I made up instead of something I was called to do. As an artist I feel it's important to capture and illustrate the many variations of life. There are so many sides to orate and shades to paint one couldn't cover them all in a lifetime, however I do my best to relate what's going on with me personally as well as the world around me. This is secondary to my purest heart's desire for all to have an everlasting encounter with the one true, living, holy and sovereign God that will impact and inspire them to reconcile with their enemies, repent for their sins, surrender their soul, and accept salvation to start a new. With this concept embedded in my soul my ministry is similar to the Apostle Paul's statement in Romans where he said, "I have became all things to all men that I might win one," and my methodology relates to the ministry of Christ himself where he would meet people exactly where they were. He evangelized to fishermen speaking about fishing, communicating in the language they best understood and ultimately receiving the best results possible. When ministering to farmers he did they same thing except he spoke in their language of seeding and harvest. This is my justification of going hard, while ministering to the urban community I engage them with the same terminology and concepts from the very lifestyles they lead in the current culture.

    I personally believe that in order to assist in the liberation of my peers who are enslaved by 'the game,' which is the same oppressor who once held me in captivity. First we must acknowledge the seriousness of the state that they're in and help them to see it also without passing judgment while displaying the obvious need for change. Secondly find a commonality, a shared place or point through experience that your lives seem to intersect. Somewhere you've been that makes you feel like the person you're ministering to could've been you or could've been in a worse position. This revelation or correlation between the parties usually creates a bond that becomes the foundation of the entire relationship. Most people are more inclined to listen to or follow a leader who can relate to or reminds them of themselves. That's why it's hard for many churches to attract and maintain members of this current generation and modern day culture. Typically one must be transparent enough to share their real testimony so that the sought after can understand their not alone in the struggle, compassionate enough to get close to them and not pass judgment while identifying with their struggle, secure enough that you don't relapse yourself in the midst of helping them because it's harder to respect someone who's doing the same thing you're doing wrong, yet strong enough to minister, witness, pray and intercede on their behalf until God breaks the chains and frees them. By people being able to relate to and believe the history of the past roads you travelled while at the same time witnessing you demonstrate your growth, maturity, and elevation it's almost inevitable to invoke change. As the world renowned powerful soul singer the late Sam Cooke would sing "… a change gon' come / Oh, yes it is / …," and keeping that song in heart, I press forward to labor for the change that God requires from us. As the old saying goes, "Be the change that you want to see in the world!"

My prayer is that my name is remembered by the Lord and when I reach the end of this journey it is called by the angels taking attendance from the book of life. Nothing is more important than this because at the end of the road if salvation and heavenly access isn't received then all I am and have done is for not! Yes I want to be remembered in the world but as a beacon of light who consistently attempted to illuminate a very dark world. May my life and legacy represent positivity, hope, peace, and the spirit of God's awesome powers of redemption, truth, and love! Remember my art form as it relates to poetic expression or lyrical capability as you did the legendary Tupac Shakur who in my personal opinion is the greatest lyricist of all-time. His music transcended ages, nations, creeds, genres, etc. He was bigger than Hip-Hop! An actor, author, activist, poet who despite where he came from or lifestyle he chose to lead, there's still memorials resurrected in his name/image, and college universities with courses dedicated to studying his writings. Let me be remembered in the Earth as a unifier of all people like you remember the honorable Dr. Martin Luther King Jr. A man who lived, fought and died for his convictions and beliefs, preaching God's holy word and the unification of all God's children regardless of sex, race, color, or creed. Even in the lieu of death he stood firmly and delivered what is remembered as the, "I Have a Dream," speech under the concept that we all are created equal. There may be a lot of progressives, communists, and people who people who believe in Eugenics to name a few that may disagree with me but just as did MLK I share in labor because I believe whole heartedly in the same dream. That's right, remember my name as you remember the late great Malcolm X, as someone who loved people and took so much pride in who he was that failure or surrendering was not an option. A man's man and a family man who was also a soldier that stood confidently on the principles. "We know our inalienable human rights, and we will protect them and ourselves by any means necessary!"

Without fear but in faith I will fight for those who can't fight for themselves and will fight alongside of those who can and will. You just make sure remember my name! After I'm gone, may the work ethic of my ministry be remembered in all the Earth as the memory of Harriet Tubman taking countless covert missions of salvation, back and forth through the land of the oppressor who wants nothing less than me captured, dead or alive? However as long as I'm physically able and there's one more soul to be saved I'm coming back to lead them North for freedom. Risking it all, every time, for each one because I'm faithful and I love God's children that much. So in closing please remember my name, remember my name as you'll forever remember the name Barack Obama and the themes of his presidential campaigns. That I might stand, live, fight and die for a 'change' in the Earth that you can believe in. May my legacy be a sign of hope so inspirational that another soldier rises up behind me and takes their rightful place in the good fight? Remember my name as a leader of the free world, a family man, and a fighter for fairness amongst all people. May I be the one who can and does when they said I can't and wouldn't. If it's in God's will my name will leave a legacy so powerful that it rings throughout history for future generations to research and witness the breaking of records, the changing of history and the world as we knew it in our time!

"Into the sunshine out of the rain and just like I did it before I'm a do it again / in this game call me Barack when you looking for change / no matter what you gon' remember my name! /…"

-SaMajesty Starr

Chapter 12 "It's On!!!"

The title "It's On," is basically a commencement of the entire album. I say that because a graduation commencement is usually a ceremony that takes place at the end of the scholastic year. Yet it also represents the beginning of another phase of life. Therefore the duplicity of the concept serves as a celebratory transition of the end, only to embark on a journey of a new beginning. As the last song on the Face 2 Face album, the idea was for whatever song selected to make a bold statement of concluding the project. Putting the official stamp on the package and sending it off. Saying that finally this phase or process is complete, and by all means it's adequate enough to stand against any other title, with a bigger name or following. While at the same time, it serves as a testament that there's so much more to come that will prove to be better than the latter, I accept all invitations for challenge or contest, and I'm ready for whatever backlash or ridicule that lies ahead. I guess the proper way to state this where I'm from would be. Don't get it twisted, this is only the beginning, but "It's On" and there's no looking back from here!

I know for some people, especially those of you who lack self-confidence or don't understand the value of self. This concept may be harder to grasp so, allow me to elaborate a little more in hopes to vividly paint a picture that carves a signature imprint of understanding into your consciousness. To begin, first I want you to think of something that you were always scared to do, that you finally faced and decided to do for the first time? It could be anything from dating to learning how to ride your bike without training wheels. Can you remember the feeling of wanting to learn but too afraid to try? Can you remember finally gathering up the courage to try and failing horribly? Now put all of those memories to the side and focus on the one time, that you got the hang of it, finally knew you could do it and said, "I got this"! If you can understand that analogy then the original concept of this final chapter/song should be remedial to your mind.

To better illustrate my point, I'll describe my first experience going free falling. I can start by mentioning the almost crippling anxiety that was boiling in the pit of my belly and the intestinal knots that accompanied it. I began profusely perspiring from everywhere and my heart rate accelerated like the speedometer in an automobile dashboard when you stand on the gas pedal! I remember climbing each and every one of those eighty-one stairs, reluctantly one foot in front of the other. Trying to comfort or reason with myself saying things like, this is nothing, we've survived much worse, be courageous and "Breathe!" Praying that the self-encouragement would calm my uneasy nerves, in an effort to release some pressure from my chest, that was tightening by the second and feeling as if it could implode at any moment! Yet I continued to put one foot in front of the other! Although each step seemed to ascend further into the deep blue, cloud-filled sky. I reminded myself not to look down on the Earth, that I felt was leaving me as the landscape widened, the items on it became further away and more of a blur. Silently I quoted all of the inspirational scriptures that I could remember, while simultaneously trying NOT to think about the ones like, "Thou shall not tempt the Lord our God!" Reciting scriptures always helps, however the time seemed to pass quicker by conversing about random topics of small talk and engaging in horseplay with the instructor who led the way. From the perspectives of other people I've spoken with and my own personal experiences in life, I just expected for the challenge to become harder the further I got into it.

Ironically the very last step, contrary to popular belief wasn't the hardest. It was the easiest! I glanced back over the last seventy-nine steps I had already climbed, looking down at the last one before stepping onto the platform, and began rejoicing like I had accomplished the goal. "I MADE IT!" Is what I began shouting from over sixty feet in the air, with my arms fully extended upright in a victorious stance and for that brief two minutes; It felt as if the whole world stood still, just to celebrate with me in that moment. There wasn't anything that could bring me down! At least until I realized that where I was standing, wasn't the initial or intended final destination and with that understanding came a sobering spirit that turned every ounce of elation in to anxiety and focus.

"You ready?" That was the question asked by the instructor that seemed to sound off in my head like a fire alarm drill. As, I stepped closer and closer to the edge of the platform I was having thoughts like, "What if this vest flies open? Or the safety cord snaps?" However no matter what kind of excuses I conjured up in my head, there was a gut feeling in the pit of my belly that spoke to my internal instincts with conviction. Matter of fact just by reminiscing about that day, I can hear that same voice repeating the same phrase continuously in my mind. "I've come too far to turn back, and GIVING UP IS NOT AN OPTION!" The totally ironic, yet sad part of the whole ordeal was even with all that power brewing inside of me, I still was stagnant!

After a few minutes of contemplation and trying to psyche myself up, I finally got to the point where I told myself ***"It's On"*** and with that mentality, in the symbolism of Jesus on the cross, I stretched my arms out wide and threw my head back. There wasn't anything else to be said, so silently, without warning, I extended my calves until I was standing on my tip toes and jumped off the edge of the platform into mid-air. I can't fathom the words to describe the major adrenaline rush that shot through my entire body, as I proved the law of gravity to be accurate by experience, slicing through wind barriers, until I suddenly felt a holy angel tackle me in mid-air and carry me to the ground. That was how it felt anyway! However in reality, it was the resistance from the bungee cord doing what it was made to do. This is what stopped me from plummeting to the ground and slowly lowered my body the rest of the way.

I didn't at that specific point in my life, but now I know my Achilles heel! Therefore, I'm going to break this down and make it personal for you. As a disclaimer, please understand my intent is only to influence you to do some soul searching, think introspectively and question if the concept of this song/chapter could be applicable in your own life. Now that the disclaimer is out of the way, let's go DEEPER!!!

With all that power you got inside of you, what's holding you back? Or even more importantly, why is it holding you back? I pose this question rhetorically from an hindsight position because, at the time I couldn't even muster up the courage to just let go and do as the title of the hobby suggest; FREELY FALL! I stood right there, scooting my size 10 black and blue leather Nike basketball shoes, to the edge of that two-foot wide platform. That was made of old worn down wood, suspended over 60ft in the air and all that I had to do was let go and Jump! Although verbally this concept seems simplistic at best, I can personally attest to the degree of difficulty involved when one attempts to manifest this simple and practical concept into his/her own individual reality. Especially when you take in to consideration the human factor, which depending on the person this could be a variable that drastically changes the whole equation. For instance, you may've had a really bad experience involving a stair case in your life and I may suffer from Acrophobia. This would be two very different circumstances from two totally different people, yet both parties would be reluctant to jump off of the same platform I stood on and would possibly require two totally different forms of motivation to do so.

"What's holding you back?" Is asking for you to find that very thing that's keeping you from doing whatever it is that you know you're supposed to be doing. After identifying and/or isolating the problem, the next question that you should present yourself with, is the infamous WHY? This is a very important question that's crucial to success, because mistakes will be made in everything you choose to do in life. However when you can understand the reason "why" the mistake happened, you can then formulate a solution to the "why", and ultimately a solution for the problem, or at bare minimum a diversion from the problem.

    The purpose of utilizing that experience was simply an attempt to convey a message of understanding. Sometimes in life you may voluntarily or involuntarily find yourself in a position, where you've come too far to turn around and yet you're scared, timid, or just having some reservations about moving forward. This could be something you've never done before? Or something you have, but the circumstances surrounding it are different. From personal experience typically this is also something BIG that you can't do alone. Yet, you're the only one who can do it! Every mistake, setback, obstacle and hurdle that comes your way, remember this is just another one of those eighty-one stairs you have to climb in order to reach the platform! Regardless of what you're going through emotionally or mentally because the anxiety/fear of the process can also have physical repercussions. This is where Old School phrases like, "You're going to worry yourself sick" derived from. I literally thought about the free fall so much, my thoughts festered into a plague of destructive emotions that morphed into a virus which, infected my internal organs and ultimately produced the physical symptoms of an illness. **"I became scared sick literally!"** Yet I continued to press my way up those stairs, encouraging myself and trying to stay preoccupied with positive affirmations mentally. "It's On!" This is what you should be telling yourself, confidently as you ascend over each stair in your life. Just to make it to the platform that has the potential to hold the greatest opportunity for success and all around growth. However don't forget this platform also presents the biggest and most difficult challenges. It is in these moments that one must rise to the occasion and overcome the emotionalism. Clinging on to the basic fabrics of their faith and screaming "It's On" the whole time!

That's how I feel about the entire "Face II Face" project. This was a mission that I was chosen to complete and even though since its inception there's been a lot of chaos and turmoil surrounding the project. Despite it all, it is my intent, obligation, and civic duty to ensure the expected, efficient and extraordinary finale. "It's on!!!"

The first step was to release all of the excuses and negative thoughts about who I am and what I can/can't do! In order to accomplish most of your biggest obstacles in life, you must first believe that you can and actually visualize yourself doing it. This is exactly the moment that you seize and own the opportunity/moment with the mentality of "It's on!" There are many spoils of war or benefits to gain from being the one who's willing to take a chance. Depending on the type of person the artist is, it could be superficial, material or even physical benefits. There are many variations to the potential benefits, due to the many variations of the human species. As for me though, it's the moment when one of your elders or someone who never really cared for "rap music" pays homage and are truly grateful for what you do. Another moment that I live for is when children consider me to be the best artist or their favorite. Not because I created the music but because I know the music is relevant, genuine and positive. I'd like to share with you one of those personal, impactful moments. {This was a blog that was copied and sent to me from an avid music listener who asked to remain anonymous.}

"FACE II FACE" the album by Samajesty Starr & A.E.

Without a question, this album exhibits the undeniable fact that it's in a class of its own! As it relates to the current industry and state of Hip-Hop, this breakout artist creates a new lane that paints a beautiful illustration for the potential of a musical revolution. It's an interesting concept and rare idea that "a rapper" could cross all genres, races and age groups. Proving that hip-hop isn't dead, if a new generation artist could be true to Hip-Hop and its roots of origin, without being vulgar, belligerent, or disrespectful to listeners and themselves. It is a very bold, yet risky move financially for an independent label to make, considering the current trend and direction that the Hip-Hop genre is moving in right now. This album displays the potential of conscious, positive, and or spiritual Rap being lucrative, relevant, and effective in the advocacy for change. It also publicizes the musical, spiritual, and personal growth of SaMajesty/Klypto which is phenomenal! It leaves audiences in a spirit of expectancy while raising the bar of skill, positivity and professionalism in the music industry as a whole. I guess what I'm saying is, "If the sky is the limit, the only question that remains for this artist is, at what altitude does he want to fly?"

  This instantly became one of those significant moments in my life because this listener not only heard the music, but felt my heart and seen the vision behind what I'm called to do. As the leader and visionary behind this project, and a pioneer of this revolutionary musical movement, I'm anxious to see what greatness is yet to follow this trail that's already blazing. How about you? Would you like to witness or be a part of something so magical, it could change the world as we know it? If so, understand that nothing worth having comes easily nor without pain and sacrifice! I dare you to stand up and accept the challenge of going against the grain! Grab a hold of your dream, vision or whatever that thing is that you know you're supposed to do and take ownership of it.

After completing this album in 2010 while still residing in Louisville, I got a message from the Lord. He spoke to my spirit and said that it was time to relocate. We needed to enlarge our territory, by taking our talents out of our comfort zone and into a new region.

For over a year I became the prophet Jonah, wrestling with this word and basically running from it, because it was uncomfortable and honestly it wasn't something that I personally wanted to do. For most people who only knew of me by my talents, couldn't understand why I was so reluctant to follow the promise of God and live my dreams. It's complicated to explain, but first you must understand that most of my kinfolk reside in the Kentuckiana area. Amongst these kinfolk, includes my first born daughter (Amore) who was conceived in a previous relationship and since getting married it has been one challenge after another, rebuilding our relationship and repairing the existing one with her mother. Just as collectively we were on the brink of cohabitation God spoke and told me to relocate. I knew that as hard as it would be for me to transition, it would be ten times harder for my baby girl who was nine years old at the time. Not to mention, together my wife and I had labored for the past five years building a brand in Da' City. We were just becoming popular for what we do, receiving all types of public notoriety, and slowly but surely prospering there, so picking up and leaving to start over just wasn't something that I logically seen as a wise move. To make matters worse we had recently got married and had two small children of our own that only proved to add more challenges to an already fragile situation. Moving to a new place where we didn't really know anybody and having to set up provisions for two toddlers just seemed like more of a challenge than I wanted to face. What was even harder to face, was the fact that I would have to separate them from their sister and most of their kinfolk. When on many occasions it was the family who assisted us in times of financial turmoil or watched the kids while we worked and chased our dreams. The situation involving Amore stuck out the most. Although it was possible that I could never salvage the intimate relationship with her mother. The thought of her having to grow up without her father in the house, or even in the region was just not something I personally agreed with. Out of all the excuses I could give you for not immediately obeying God's word, this was definitely the most influential one. For these reasons and maybe one or two other more selfish reasons that we will be omitting from the story, I fought against the constant voice of the Lord saying, "You have to go, relocate and expand your territory!" Eventually, I learned that you can't fight against the words of God! Within a year my wife and I suffered more hardships and pain than we had the whole time we had been together. Of everything that was lost in my disobedience nothing rocked the very foundations of my manhood like the baby we lost by miscarriage. It was in that vulnerable, pain filled place of brokenness that I completely surrendered to his will and knew what I had to do.

The very next Sunday while attending a morning worship service at Elim Baptist Church, the pastor Reverend Vincent James preached a sermon that was based around following your dreams and doing something different. In which he said, "I don't know who you are but God has been dealing with you for a long time now about relocation and you're expecting more from God but you're not willing to try something different!" Needless to say, but the word that went forth that Sunday was for me and I received it. I stopped trying to fight against the will of God and I tried something different. I got up and relocated my family and didn't stop until I was told to, which ended up being Columbia, SC. I'm overwhelmingly grateful that I serve a God who keeps his promises and makes provisions for those who believe in his promises. I can't begin to name all of the angels, friends and extended family I've been blessed with on this journey. It wasn't easy and there were some times that were so rough I questioned if I ever heard from God in the first place. However the good most definitely outweighed the bad and having somebody there, almost every time you needed someone has definitely made the transition smoother than anticipated. Each and every one of you knows who you are and what you mean to me without having your name called. I say thank you! I've been blessed in a multitude of ways that never would've happened if I didn't have the courage to be obedient, do something different and relocate! Andre C. Barnes authored an excellent book that solidifies my overall sentiments at that time. "Can't go back, Can't stay here, what's up over there?" I find that my life parallels the story he wrote, speaking of how everything one might need could be right there waiting for you, if you have the courage to do something different and go get it!

Last but not least, I was given the task by God to sit down and author my first book. This was something that I always wanted to do but felt like I just couldn't. I'm not sure to what extent or level of blessings this book will provide for my family and ministry. However, I do know that personally it has provided me with a new level of understanding and respect for myself, compassion and grace to minister to and for others, as well as an accelerated drive and passion to please the Lord. After all I've been through, I'm learning that nothing can stop me or hold me back, except me! There is something different about me but I've learned to embrace it and utilize those same things to propel me forward because I actually have something to offer.

I might be from ***Da' City*** where most of the time, you'll hear more negative than positive, and way too many great people get stuck and never make it out. However to hear me speak, listen to my music, or to read my writings, you can't help but feel in your heart the connect with me in spirit knowing that ***This is for you***! There is a glow in my aura and a passion in my soul that goes forth like a ***Fire***, and I know that it can't all be me. Therefore, I'm not ashamed to acknowledge and proclaim God, ***It was You***. After all I didn't choose this path, it chose me! Trying to avoid my destiny, I walked right into it and began creating ***My Legacy.*** I became a true fan of life and living it, I just hope you realize that life is very short, so celebrate it like ***It's Ya Birthday***! I refused to be put in a box, so quit trying to box me in and ***Gimme Some Room*** to just be me. I can manage my own affairs and I don't need any help deciding what's ***Perfect*** for me. When I was presented with the same ***Ultimatum*** that you were given, I decided that I was ***Goin All Out,*** and after the smoke clears and the dust settles, YOU WILL ***Remember My Name***!!! As one who stood and fought for what he believed in, with faith not fear, and faced every challenge eye to eye, screaming ***It's On!!!***

2 Fingers (Peace) and 1 God (Love)
-Samajesty Starr

About the Author

Sammy D. Vaughn III

Sammy D. Vaughn III also known as (A.E.) Klypto or better known as Samajesty Starr is the second eldest of five children. Born in Columbus, Georgia but raised in Louisville KY. This is where his passionate pass time of ciphering lyrics would later turn into a full fledge musical career. Following the footprints of his father who was a D.J; Sammy began listening, and mixing, various genres of music with his new found love for hip-hop.

Around the tender age of ten he began rapping and performing with a group of his cousins under the name MADDHOUSE, which was formed by his cousin and mentor the late Lamonte Hardcore Silver. Word quickly traveled the streets about the music and Sam was introduced to Robert Hayes aka Black Godfather and joined the then up and coming Winner Take All Entertainment Camp. Where he recorded his first album God Understand Me, under the alias Klypto (Clepto).

While the album was never released Sammy wrote and recorded songs on the Nationally Released Soundtrack Winner Take All from the motion picture Winner Take All which premiered on the BET network and gave Sam his introduction to the art form of acting. After learning that soon he would become a father Sam then began strengthening his relationship in his Baptist Christian faith. Still dedicated to the music he began writing, performing and ministering the Gospel with a hip-hop twist under the name Samajesty Starr.

Once again word traveled fast and Sam quickly became a hometown favorite performing for over 50 churches and 20 schools in the Greater Louisville area. Writing material for and/or performing for organizations such as Simmons College of Louisville, Future Promotions Professional Boxing @ Expo 5, WAVE TV 3: Dare to Care Food Drive, The Louisville Youth Opportunity Network, WHAS TV :Great Day Live Morning Show, Ms. Neal and the Rockettes Dance Company, Office of Council Woman Judith Greene, Kentucky Cabinet for Domestic Violence, Light Up Louisville and became a regular on Power104.3 with J HAZZ. Sam recently received a Proclamation from Louisville Mayor Greg Fischer, declaring February 10, 2013 Sammy Vaughn Day. After being on tour for a couple years as Samajesty, Sam now feels he has found what he likes to call the balance in music. The Balance is to give all of me without loosing me, says Samajesty Starr. bv

Preparing to write his debut hip-hop album Face 2 Face he shut himself off from the outside world for two months. He emerged with the Greater Louisville Anthem Da City, as well as the WHAS Crusade for Children sponsored single, This is For You. One thing Sam takes pride in about his music is its sincere and you can feel the sincerity vibe in the energy behind his lyrics live or on disc. His music defies the categorical laws of genres, his lyrics penetrate the soul of man and raises questions.

The past four years Sam has been devoted to using his gift of music and creative arts to bring communities together. While in Louisville he started a campaign to save the street of Louisville. Mayor Greg Fischer of Louisville Kentucky gave Sammy a proclamation, declaring February 10, 2013 Sammy Vaughn Day for his outstanding service in the community. In 2013 he and his family relocated to Columbia South Carolina to open their horizons in the music field. It was here that he obtained a group name of AS-1. The group is a dynamic duo consisting of him and his wife Queen Cherrie. Since there, they have worked with BUDS Mentoring Services, Twinkle Toes Dance Studio, Blue Fire Video Productions Company, Palmetto Youth, J.U.M.P.S Program, Mt. Hermon, The Vertical Lounge and Many more. They had the chance to compete in the Charleston Black EXPO in which they won 1st place in their division. Benedict College Grammy Awards Show, they were one of the featured artists. The list goes on and on. His motto is that he can change the world with his gift and that is what he plans to do!

Download My Album

http://www.cdbaby.com/cd/samajestystarraeklypto

Pure Thoughts Publishing, LLC

www.PureThoughtsPublishingLLC.com

www.ingramcontent.com/pod-product-compliance
Lightning Source LLC
LaVergne TN
LVHW011203080426
835508LV00007B/575